IN HER SHOES

STEP BY STEP

MADONNA DRIES CHRISTENSEN

iUniverse, Inc.
Bloomington

In Her Shoes
Step by Step

iUniverse books may be ordered through booksellers or by contacting:

iUniverse
1663 Liberty Drive
Bloomington, IN 47403
www.iuniverse.com
1-800-Authors (1-800-288-4677)

Front Cover Photo: Madonna, Maybelle holding Shirley, circa 1938

ISBN: 978-1-4759-2870-9 (sc)
ISBN: 978-1-4759-2871-6 (e)

Library of Congress Control Number: 2012909322

Printed in the United States of America

iUniverse rev. date: 6/26/2012

For my daughter, Jill,
and her children:
Grace Linnet
Sarah Catherine
William Lancaster

From my German heritage—
Dein ist mein ganzes herz.
(You are my heart's delight.)

From the Gaelic—
Grandchildren are *ceol binn*.
(sweet music)

And as my French-speaking grandfather might have said:
Ma Cherie.

Royalties from sales of this book and three of my previous books are donated to Down Syndrome Association of Northern Virginia.

To those who love children with special needs. Heaven knows your sacrifice and holds your reward.

~ ~ Robert Whitlow

Table Of Contents

COLLECTED MEMOIRS

<u>The Early Years</u>

The Man With A Grin

The Forties And Fifties Merge

Christmas Collective

Stepping Into Her Shoes

RELATIVELY SPEAKING

PIECE WORK

FINALE

PREFACE

As a child, my daughter sometimes requested at bedtime, "Tell me a story about when you were a little girl." Quite likely some of my stories involved my father and mother. At some point it occurred to me that I knew precious little about my parents. I was in high school when my father died and had barely come of age when my mother died, so I had a limited point of view. Some of us in the family didn't know until my mother's death that her given name was Agnes Isabella. She was Maybelle to family and friends.

Over the years, my parents' absence left me feeling cheated. I wanted my daughter and her future children to know more about me than I'd known about my parents. That realization started me on the road to genealogy; in search of my parents through photographs, documents, letters, newspaper articles, and other people's view of them.

Genealogy led to memoir writing. At age fifty, my first submission was published simultaneously in the *Arlington* (Virginia) *Journal* and the *Osceola County* (Iowa) *Gazette Tribune*. I'd been reticent about submitting. Shy as a child and teenager, I remained guarded when speaking about myself. Being published brought the realization that I possibly had something of interest to say. Through writing, I had a voice.

Still, I had plenty to learn, not only about the process of writing but about the business end of it. One or two accepted manuscripts do not a writer make. Step by step, piece by piece, I created a body of work that has appeared in scores of publications across the country and in Canada, including *Good Old Days, Reminisce, Horizon Magazine, Nostalgia, Yesterday's Magazette*, the *Tampa Tribune, Catholic Digest,* the *Washington Post,* the *Sarasota Herald-Tribune, Clever Magazine,* and *The Elder Storytelling Place*. Also, in a dozen or more anthologies, including *The Writer,* and in two by Silver Boomer Books: *From the Porch Swing: memories of our grandparents,* and *The Harsh and The Heart: Celebrating the Military*. When the guidelines arrived from the editor for an upcoming book on widowhood, I replied that I'd have to pass on submitting to this one; that I'm not a widow. She responded, "You're a writer. It doesn't have to be about you."

That comment opened a door to a subject I'd never explored on paper: *How my mother's widowhood and her subsequent death profoundly shaped my life*. The resulting submission to Silver Boomer Books prompted me to publish this compilation, with *In Her Shoes* as the theme.

This book is not autobiography, which covers a person's full life and is factual (some folks have toyed with that). This is memoir, individual stories about a particular time of one's life, *as he or she remembers it*. Since this collection is an attempt to know and understand my parents, the settings do not go much beyond childhood, because those are the only years I shared with them—the only place I can find them (Ashton/ Sibley, Iowa).

Although what I've written is, in theory, the way I remember it, I drew on other's recall. My two next in age older brothers and I shuffled individual pieces of a particular puzzle until a probable picture appeared.

Memoir is both difficult and fun. Difficult because many elements of a particular event are lost to time; fun because hindsight and perspective come into play. Writers take literary license to create dialogue and inner thoughts of how it probably was or might have been.

I did not sit down and start writing from scratch; most of the stories were written over the past twenty-five years. They are not in chronological order by my age; childhood does not occur in order; it is of an era, without much transition from one day or month or year to the next. Most of the stories were previously published individually, so details as to setting or year are sometimes repeated. I eliminated what I could, but for the most part, deleting material mars the clarity of a particular story. I hope you will bear with the repetition. Where vintage letter excerpts are used, they are as written, including errors and words that are now considered not *politically correct*. I sometimes added a word or two, in brackets, for clarification.

Writer Anne Lamott says she once submitted a memoir manuscript to a publisher who replied, "You've made the mistake of thinking that everything about your life is interesting."

Ah, yes; *it is* presumptuous to publish a memoir or autobiography. Moreover, for me, it's somewhat out of character. I relish and respect privacy. But as stated earlier, I broke the shell of timidity. The result is an outpouring of stories. Blame it on age; it's now or never to have my say.

Elmore Leonard and James Patterson, whose style is spare, advise writers to leave out the parts that readers only scan or skip altogether. Memoir cannot be completely cleansed of family history, but I tried to separate the two. The beginning section is memoir. Stories that are more clearly family history are in a section called Relatively Speaking. That's followed by

Piece Work, which is more nostalgia than memoir. Please use your own literary license to scan and skip.

I thank you for reading *In Her Shoes*. All or part of it.

Madonna Dries Christensen
<u>Iowagirl1@aol.com</u>

Gary and Madonna, circa 1937

ACKNOWLEDGMENTS

Frank Anton Dries (Poppy)	1896-1952
Agnes Isabella Guertin (Maybelle/Ma)	1903-1957
Joseph Edgar	1922-1995
Vincent Elmer	1923-1982
Sybella Rose (Billie)	1925-2012
Dolores Mae (Lorcy)	1926-2001
Norma Ann (Toots)	1928-1943
Merlyn Francis (Mike)	1930-2006
Daryl Edward	1932-
Gary Eugene	1934-
Madonna Joy	1935-
Shirley Jane	1937-
Lawrence Franklin	1939-2004
Daniel Lee	1941-2010
Donald Thomas	1944-1945
Dennis Michael	1945-
David Patrick	1945-1996

I'm grateful for my past family, my current family, and friends too numerous to list. My life is blessed with the luck of the Irish.

Special hugs to Shirley, my partner in childhood adventure.

Maybelle, Joe, Frank, circa 1942

INTRODUCTION

When I was eight, and my father was recovering from a heart attack, someone gave him a used jigsaw puzzle in a box with no cover. As I helped with the puzzle I complained about having no picture to guide us. I don't recall Poppy's exact words but it was something like, "We'll keep at it, piece by piece, and the picture will appear."

I now view that memory as a metaphor for life; it evolves piece by piece, section by section. We don't know what will emerge along the way, nor what the completed image will be.

By age seventeen, my personal picture revealed an average student with a part-time job at J.C. Penney. If I could have seen more, I might have been frightened by what lay ahead—by the chain of events that would define my early adult life.

In December of that year, 1952, my mother became a widow. Married for thirty-one years, she had given birth to fifteen children. I hear gasps from readers, but large families were common in those days, especially among Catholics and farm folks. We were both. With twenty-three years between the oldest and youngest, we were never all under the same roof together as children.

I don't recall my mother's state of mind following my father's death. His funeral was a week before Christmas. The youngest children were twin boys, age seven, and a boy age eleven, so I assume we had a semblance of holiday cheer for their benefit.

In a letter my older sister saved, Ma wrote, "It don't seem possible it will soon be a month since your dad is gone. It still seems like a dream. I miss him most from 5:00 on." (The time he had come home from work.)

She carried on with dignity, determination, and faith. In addition to her salary as a café cook, there were my father's Social Security and veteran's benefits for each minor child. Those of us old enough to work earned our pocket money. Ma made payments on my father's funeral bill until it was paid. Poppy had ruled that we didn't need a telephone or a television set. Ma purchased both. She enjoyed television and chatting on the phone with her sister, Goldie. They lost their mother in 1955, and Goldie was widowed, too.

That same year, my two years younger sister and I moved to Sioux Falls, South Dakota, about an hour away. Ma argued against our going, but we reasoned that we could find better jobs there and could send money home. Alas, we lived paycheck to paycheck and I don't recall sending money home. I later realized that Ma needed our company and emotional support at home, too. To be fair to Shirley and me, we were unaware when we left home that Ma's health was fragile.

We'd been away a year when Ma had a small stroke. She needed to give up her job and not do anything strenuous. Shirley had become engaged and made plans to move to the town where her fiancé was in college. I returned home to help, and resumed working at Penney's.

The following April, in 1957, my mother died, leaving three minor sons, now ages eleven and fifteen. When one of the twins commented that they would have to go to the orphanage, I assured him that wouldn't happen. With that response, a decision had been made.

Or was it a decision? Was there an alternative road down which I could walk away? My married siblings were raising families and Shirley planned to marry next year. That left me.

When I told a co-worker that I was going to be my brothers' legal guardian, she said, "Oh, my, you can't do that."

I was taken aback. Of course I could do it. We had a house to live in (rented from my uncle); I had a job, and the Social Security and veteran's benefits would continue. My two older brothers stayed home, too. The dynamics had changed, but the household continued operating.

Two years later, the oldest of my charges graduated from high school. Being independent and resourceful, Danny left home to work and put himself through art school in Minneapolis. In Sibley, a small town, I had little social life; my female friends were in college, married, or had moved away. Dating was sporadic, with no one who tethered me to a future in the homeplace. I moved with the twins to Sioux Falls, where I had siblings and friends, and I returned to the job I'd previously held at Brown and Saenger Office Supplies.

In the early 1960s, *the times they were a changin'*. The rapidly shifting values made those of my teen years Victorian by comparison. Although my brothers were respectful to me, there were serious problems. During one troublesome period, one older brother came to lend a hand.

In retrospect, I understand what my friend meant when she said I couldn't become guardian to three minor boys. As a mother herself, she was suggesting there was more to raising children than keeping a roof over their heads. She was right, of course. With hindsight, I wish I'd handled certain situations differently, but given my age and life experience to that point, I did the best I knew how. I can't rewrite that chapter. That would mean rewriting the entire book and I have no desire to deny, alter, diminish, or embellish any part of my life. I'm content with *then* and *now*. We become who we are because of who we were; a culmination of the momentous and the minutiae.

Although I stepped into my mother's shoes, I didn't fill them. But with the memory of her dedication to family and her indomitable Irish spirit guiding me, I stumbled through seven years of surrogate motherhood.

It was not a choice; it was simply the right thing to do.

Dennis, Madonna, David, circa 1963

{ COLLECTED MEMOIRS }

The Early Years

Longing To Know Her

Gone—flitted away;
Taken the stars from the night and the sun
From the day!
Gone, and a cloud in my heart.

~ ~ Alfred Tennyson

In vintage photos, Agnes Isabella (Maybelle) Guertin, age six, wears a white ruffled dress; a white bow in her dark pipe curls. She is angelic, a French Canadian/Irish beauty. The sepia photo does not reveal it, but her eyes are soft gray.

Age ten, with her family, another white dress, black stockings. Maybelle is somber. A professional photographer is serious business.

Age ten, again a white dress, she and her brother straddle a fence around a pigpen, while their father works beside them.

Age eleven, a school group photo, Maybelle chose a black dress, long black stockings, and black high-button shoes. She holds hands with a blonde girl. In the front row, a student holds a slate on which is written; Guertin School, 1914. Country schools were named for the person on whose land the school sat; in this case, my great-grandfather, Zebulon Eugene Francis Guertin.

The two school girls, now teenagers, their hair fashionably bobbed, smile as they pose with a tree trunk between them, their hands clasped together around the tree. The picture speaks one word: Friendship.

"Maybelle was kind of shy, but she had lots of friends," my uncle tells me when I ask what my mother was like as a child.

June 14, 1921, petite, eighteen-years-old; the newspaper wedding announcement states that the bride was becomingly gowned in a white crepe meteor dress and a white hat. The photo reveals white stockings and white pumps, but no hat. Maybelle sits beside the handsome groom, Frank Dries, age twenty-five, on separate chairs. Her hands, resting on a shower bouquet of bridal roses, display a diamond ring and a plain gold band. Around her neck, a crucifix on a chain. The wedding announcement states that the groom, wearing "the usual blue serge" is "well and favorably known in this community, he having grown to adulthood in our midst. He is a prosperous and industrious farmer." Maybelle looks frightened. None of the foursome in the wedding party is smiling. Marriage is serious business.

A year later, stylish in a black coat, black cloche, black stockings, black shoes, Maybelle stands on the Iowa farmhouse porch, holding her first-born child, Joseph Edgar, named for his two grandfathers.

The farmer's wife poses behind a team of horses, reins in her hands. Her dark curls are covered by a man's felt hat, the brim shading her eyes from the sun. A loose apron over a Mother Hubbard dress does not conceal her second pregnancy. There will be many more.

"Maybelle loved babies. She'd walk for miles to see a new baby," my aunt tells me when I ask what my mother was like as a girl.

Through the years Maybelle controls the Kodak box camera, documenting the lives of her children as they multiply. There are few photos of her; now and then she appears. My younger sister and I sit with her in a meadow. She stands in the yard with my father and their oldest son, soon leaving for World War II. She and I pose together in the snow, squinting into the sun. She sits on the lawn with my brother, the two of them shelling peas from the garden. She peeks from behind a pine tree, hiding from the camera. One Sunday morning, she is spiffy in a navy blue suit and hat.

The years pass, her girlish figure gone, she is photographed with twin boys, her last born. The family gathers on Christmas day for a professional group photo in which we all smile goofily at the camera.

Soon, my father disappears from the pages of the family album. Ma is grateful for the group photo; there are only two showing all of us together.

Before long she is gone; in her sleep. In a picture in her coffin, she wears a gray dress with red trim, chosen by my older sisters. They like the touch of red. They tell me, "Poppy didn't like her to wear bright colors. He thought they were flirtatious."

Long years later, still missing the mother who never grew old, I covet the silent images in pictures. I study her eyes, her smile, her frown; her body language. I strain to hear her voice, trying to understand who she was—longing to know her.

Frank and Maybelle, Leon Guertin, Rose Dries, 1921

Frank and Maybelle, 1921

A Scrap Of Time And Place

We are all visitors to this time, this place. We are only passing through. Our purpose here is to observe, to learn, to grow, to love, and then we return home.

~ ~ Australian Aborigine proverb

Aunt Goldie beamed like the matchmaker Yenta when she said, "They met at my house."

I had asked my mother's older sister how my parents met. She passed me a plate of brownies and explained.

She didn't actually lay claim to arranging the meeting; it appears to have been coincidental. Her husband, Elmer Foley, and Frank Dries met at Camp Pike, Arkansas, in 1918, young men training to be doughboys. Elmer went overseas first and Frank's troop ship set sail on November 11, the day the armistice ending the war was signed. The ship returned to port the next day; the men returned to camp, and Frank was mustered out in December. Sometime during the next year, he stopped by to see Elmer and Goldie. Sixteen-year-old Maybelle Guertin was there. The two courted, and married in 1921.

From a wedding announcement I learned that the newlyweds set up housekeeping on a farm near Ashton, one of three owned by my paternal grandfather. The couple probably did fairly well those first few years, but when my widower grandfather died in 1937, his will called for the farms to be sold and the money divided among his seven heirs. My father could not afford to buy the farm we lived on and, due to the Depression, farms did not sell quickly, so our family remained there until the farm sold in 1940. After moving to town, my father worked nights at a construction company keeping a pump operating. Later, we moved to Sibley, a few miles away, where he worked as a carpenter for a construction company. After a heart attack in 1943, needing an easier job, he became office manager for a veterinarian.

My mother sometimes reminisced about leaving the farm: "On the night before we moved to town, I found Frank sitting in the barn, crying. He had sixty-five cents in his pocket. I don't think he ever got over losing the farm. At least we had food on the table, and when things got really bad, Frank sold a pig and we got by. We struggled for years and then had to leave just about the time farmers were beginning to make a profit again."

The man who bought the farm later told my brother Daryl, "When your dad left, he took everything that wasn't nailed down. He didn't leave even a scrap of lumber."

But he did leave something; something that was found more than a half century later—a serendipitous discovery.

In 1995, on a visit to Iowa, Daryl stopped by our former farm. The dilapidated barn looked as if a strong wind and a heavy rain could make it implode. When the owner said he intended to raze the structure soon, Daryl asked permission to take a few boards for souvenirs. The owner told him to help himself.

Daryl searched inside and outside the barn, looking for pieces suitable to use as picture frames. He finally spotted a board that seemed the right size and shape. When he picked it up he noticed the letters F.D. carved into the board.

Our father's initials.

When had he done this? As a kid, trying out a pocketknife he got for Christmas? Or before he left the farm as an adult, leaving his indelible mark? We'll never know. But had Daryl gone to the farm a day later, the entire barn might have been gone, and with it the slab of board bearing those initials.

I have a piece of the weathered wood (not the initialed one) in a frame, along with a photo of the barn and a photo of the farmhouse where my father was born and raised and toiled and began a family. The collage hangs above my desk. When I sojourn in the past, the scrap of wood grounds me to a place and time that meant a great deal to my father. And to me; it's where my life began.

Maybelle, circa 1923

Here's Looking At You, Kids

A picture is worth a thousand words.

~ ~ Unknown

The oral history of a family, while valuable, tends to change as it drifts through generations. Events are viewed differently by different people; memories fade, and tales are often edited or embellished to suit the teller. Without photographs, much family history would be lost or inaccurate. Photos acquaint us with kinfolk we never knew, and keep alive the memory of those who've gone before us. They enable us to go home again and visit the past. Pictures shore up and enrich memories; fill in details when the mind fails. Pictures provide answers to genealogy questions. A license plate on a car marked Just Married identifies the year a couple wed and the state in which to find their marriage license.

My mother had her Kodak box camera handy from the first days of marriage, when she took a picture of her husband and their firstborn on the farmhouse porch. Poppy was debonair in a suit and a snap-brim cap; Joe wore baby attire, complete with high-button shoes. Then Poppy turned the camera on Ma and Joe (Poppy's shadow is visible in the photo). Ma is fashionably dressed in a cloche, a coat with a fur collar, black hose and shoes. Her hat tells me they were dressed for church; Catholic women covered their heads back then.

More children followed, and Ma's pictorial story unfolded over three decades. In the driveway at the farm, a bevy of children, along with aunts, uncles, and cousins, are piled atop and around a car, reminiscent of a scene from *The Grapes Of Wrath*.

My two oldest brothers posed atop a snow-covered farm building, verifying the mountains of snow during the blizzards of 1936-37. Tunnels were dug to the barn to feed the animals, and for thirty-eight consecutive days the temperature ranged from zero to thirty-five below.

There's a picture labeled: Christmas day, 1946, when we traipsed outdoors coatless to prove that Iowa has warm winter days. Another picture recalls for me not only my wool pants suit made from my brother's Navy uniform, but the seamstress who made it. Emma Tjossem was a tiny widow who smelled like Sen-Sen. She lived across the street from the park, upstairs in someone's house, with the outdoor flight of stairs around back. She wore a pincushion bracelet, a tape measure necklace, and a dress adorned with snippets of thread.

I know that we were as poor as the proverbial church mouse, but our apparel would not reveal that to strangers viewing our pictures. I've looked at other people's pictures from that era and my family doesn't look much different than they do. Our clothing was home sewn, from church rummage sales, and store-bought. Garments and shoes were handed down from one to the next until there wasn't an hour's worth of wear left.

We were captured in play clothes and dirty faces, and scrubbed faces and angelic white for First Communion and Confirmation. For the latter occasions the boys had fresh haircuts; their curls, cowlicks, or crew cuts slicked down or up with a comb dipped in water. We girls added veils, ribbons, or bows to our pipe-curls. We each held a new rosary draped over a new prayer book; white for girls, black for boys.

We wore feed sack dresses and pinafores, mannish little boy three piece suits, knickers, Army nurse and cowboy costumes, overalls, coveralls, sweaters, snowsuits, mackinaws, pea jackets, and coats pinned shut where buttons had been. The boys wore blue denim jeans they called "whoopee pants." I don't know why. With the jeans they wore "inner-outer" shirts. You guessed it, they could be worn tucked in or hanging out.

Our heads were capped with baby bonnets, Easter hats, ear flappers, stocking caps, headscarves, and turbans. We were shod in high-tops, oxfords, loafers, patent leather, sandals, saddle shoes, and four buckle overshoes. In winter, our knobby-kneed little girl legs were covered with full-length brown cotton stockings, wrinkled like an elephant's legs from the long johns underneath. When it grew warm, we shed the underwear and rolled the stockings into plump doughnuts around our ankles. Then we switched to anklets or bobby socks, next came bare legs and, finally, bare feet. Ah; summer had arrived.

Pictures tell me about my three older sisters as teenagers. Sometimes pudgy, other times slim, they were perky, giggly, pouty, coy, and sexy. Their hair styles and clothing reveal that they were fashion conscious. The two older girls rolled their hair in pads called "rats," or used home permanents to set it into tight curls. The youngest of the trio didn't need accouterments. Her hair was naturally curly, coal black, thick, and lustrous. When war brought a hosiery shortage, they wore leg makeup and drew seam lines up the backs of their legs. They dolled up in hats or snoods, spectator pumps, wedgies, and sling-back shoes, pleated slacks, shorts and midriffs, dirndl skirts, blouses tied under their bosoms, Rosie The Riveter overalls, and dresses whose style has come and gone again.

My younger brothers, Larry and Danny, were photographed seated in a homemade wagon, adorable in over-sized caps. A couple of years later, Ma caught the same pair, plus four friends, perched on a bench like crows on a telephone line, reading comic books. The twin babies of the family are shown doing this, that, and the other thing. Coming along in late 1945 after the deaths of two children within seventeen months, twins brought Ma's models to a baker's dozen.

Norma had died at fifteen from kidney disease; eight-month-old Donnie from pneumonia. The last picture taken of Norma belied her illness; only my parents knew she was dying. I was eight at the time, and nine-and-a-half when Donnie died. I recall their deaths, but almost nothing about their lives. Family snapshots verify their brief existence.

Ma sometimes stopped her work and our play and appeared with her camera. "Hold still a minute," she'd say, and we'd freeze like a game of statues. On one such day, when winter had conceded to spring, she posed us in the yard where the sun had melted enormous mounds of snow. The resulting picture, showing trees and houses mirrored in large puddles, was one of her favorites.

"Larry, you little devil, get away," she often said when she had a select group of us arranged just so. "I want only the girls in this picture." But like Alfred Hitchcock appearing in all his own movies, Larry played the extra in our scenes. His mug can be seen behind a bush or in the corner somewhere.

One day I asked Ma to show me how to use her camera. She handed it over and instructed, "Hold it at your waist, find the picture in the window, and push this button. The sun should be behind you. Turn this knob after every picture or you'll have a double exposure."

"Who should I take a picture of?" I asked.

"Anyone but me," she replied. She preferred being on the business end of the camera rather than the object of its curious eye.

When I began earning money of my own, in the 1950s, I bought a camera with a flash attachment. This opened new possibilities: we could be photographed inside as well as outdoors. That was about the time Ma retired her old black box, thinking, I imagine, that newer is better. Not always so. I had several cameras after that, but the color has faded from many prints taken only a few years ago. Ma's black and white images remain sharp, and continue conveying stories to her grandchildren and their children and beyond. Many are now spread across the Internet and on Facebook.

Ma could never have imagined the photographic legacy she left us. But I thank her for it whenever I sift through the treasure trove of images, all of them now digitalized and shared with several generations.

Left to right back, Madonna,
Shirley, front Danny,
Larry, circa 1946

Seated on fence, Madonna, Shirley; standing,
Dolores, Norma, Sybella, circa 1940

Stairsteps circa 1942: Joe (Vince missing),
Dolores, Sybella, Norma, Merlyn, Daryl (holding
Danny), Gary, Madonna, Shirley, Larry

Dolores holding Donny, 1944

Touching Norma

A lock of hair from a child so fair;
A miracle from above, placed gently in my care.

~ ~ Anonymous

After my sister Dolores died in 2001, her daughter, Kelli, gave me a packet of materials that Dolores had saved from when Norma Ann died in 1943, at age fifteen. I had just turned eight then. I have only flimsy memories of Norma. In one, she comes home from choir practice laughing at herself. She had to leave her coat on during practice because she'd forgotten to wear a skirt. She was wearing only a full slip and a blouse.

I have no recall of Norma being sick, but I remember the morning Ma came upstairs and woke us kids and told us we wouldn't be going to school; Norma had died. A woman came to the house with new dresses for Shirley and me to wear to the funeral, but I don't recall attending the funeral. I'm told that Poppy, having had a heart attack, could not attend, and that he had sat beside the casket in the parlor and cried. Later, he watched from the window as the casket was carried from the house and driven away.

Among the saved memorabilia there are cards and letters written to Ma and Poppy when Norma died, cards for Masses, and a list of food and other items people brought to the house.

There are cards and letters from schoolmates during the time Norma was absent from school, in Ashton and Sibley, and letters and school papers that Norma wrote.

In a letter from Shirley Wimmer (a cousin), I am mentioned, but not by name. Dated November 22, 1940, Shirley opened her letter with this comment:

Dear Norma: Camilla and I sweep Sister Bonaventure's room every noon. We help the children dress and undress. Your little sister always stands outside the school door. I guess nobody will play with her.

There's a crocheted doily that Norma made, and a drawing done in colored pencil. Although it's not labeled, I recognized the face as movie star Van Johnson. There are school papers: math/algebra, science, and English. The following excerpt is intriguing for its mystery (the first page is missing). It appears that Norma stayed out late and had an encounter with Ma, who might have been waiting, sleeping on the couch, perhaps. That would explain the first complete sentence.

N.A.D. page 2

mother. She had to make sure she caught me. With a very angry face, she queried, "What time does it happen to be?" I tried to explain but all she said before turning over was, "Remember, no more movies for you the rest of the month." She must have overlooked a certain fact that it was the 29th of the month already. So tell me don't you think I got off pretty easy?
Norma Ann Dries
English 9, Sept 17, 1943

An excerpt from another English paper—a kind of outline:

Sept 23, 1943 English 8-2 Norma Dries

Enteresting subject matter for letters: I would like to have a talk by letter with my sister-in-law Phoebe. She enjoys a more humorous letter and I would naturally include a few jokes. I would also ask her about the baby Sonya Kaye, and about her sister Marilyn. Then I would tell her about school, home, and town.

In a letter to her two older sisters, Norma is feisty, gossipy, and irreverent. She refers to Poppy as *the old man.*

Say, why did the moron jump in the banker's pocket? ans: Because the doctor told him he needed a little change.

I just went to Confession and Communion a few days ago or else I'd really tell you one.

Oh, now I thought of something else, something about Dorothy. You can imagine. I heard she quit school but I didn't think about why she did. Arlowene told Ma. She's taking after her mother I spose.

Recently, while looking through this Norma collection I ran across something I'd seen before, but not for some time. It startled me anew. A small white box holds a lock of her hair. Her hair is what captivates me when I look at photos. Her long, thick, luxurious black curls must have been the envy of her peers.

The strand is in a cellophane envelope, brittle and yellowed. Hesitant at first, I carefully slipped the hair from the wrapping. I shivered, and my eyes filled with tears.

How can touching this hair after so many years bring such emotion?

I hardly knew her.

Who clipped the curl? Ma, or Dolores?

If it was Dolores, did she do it secretly?

When was it clipped? Before Norma died, or after?

When my generation is gone, who will remember Norma Ann?

Who will want this still tangible part of her?

Who might, another 50 years from now, touch this lock of hair and be touched, as was I?

Back, Norma, left, Dolores, right, Sybella
Taken two months before Norma died

The Real Thing

He's the real Mackay.

~ ~ Robert Lewis Stevenson, 1883

We kids watched the clock, waiting for dismissal, while Sister issued her closing announcements. "Tomorrow, after school, a man from the Coca-Cola Company will be on the playground. If you bring a nickel, you can buy a bottle of Coca-Cola. However, your nickel ..." The bell interrupted and she added, "We'll talk about it tomorrow."

I'd heard of Coca-Cola, but by the time I got home my excitement about it had waned. There were five of us kids in school, and while I was not familiar with multiplication, I felt certain that five kids times five nickels was more than Poppy could spare.

Still, I hoped that one of my siblings would mention the Coca-Cola man. Sure enough, the next noon at dinner my older brothers bragged about having collected and sold enough scrap metal for a bottle apiece. My older sister, Norma, was sick and not going to school, so that left only me without funds. I said something to that effect.

The remark seemed to miss its target. Poppy said nothing. I helped clear the table, hoping my effort would be noticed and rewarded. Still nothing from the man with the money.

I had stalled as long as I could; it was time to return to school. I shuffled to the door wearing a pitiful look. I paused, and looked back.

Ma reached in her purse, and I waited while she fished out a nickel and knotted it in the corner of a handkerchief. She tied the other end to my sash and warned, "Leave it there until after school."

All afternoon the hanky hung there, as limp as a flag on a windless day. I was tempted to practice untying the knot, but in Sister's class it was not a good idea to draw attention to yourself if what you were doing was nonacademic.

Before dismissal, Sister tapped a ruler against a poster on the wall. The ruler always got our attention. Once when a boy seated behind me pulled my hair, Sister slapped his hands with the ruler. As she turned her back and returned to the front of the room, Harold whispered to me, "They're bleeding."

I had no pity; my head still stung from his tug on my hair.

Now Sister said, "Those of you who are fortunate enough to have a nickel should, in good conscience, give it to the missionaries in the Belgian Congo, for the starving pagan babies, instead of spending it on foolishness."

So that's what she'd started to say yesterday. These dark-skinned, wide-eyed children on the poster had sad faces and swollen stomachs. How could they be hungry with those big stomachs? And where was the Belgian Congo? And what did pagan mean? Whenever the pagan babies came up at home, Poppy said he had enough mouths to feed. But he usually found a coin or two, even if it was only pennies.

I hoped that Sister hadn't seen my hanky with the tell-tale nickel knotted inside. I don't know if any of my classmates succumbed to her suggestion and dropped their money in the mission box, but I know that when the bell rang and I slunk out to the playground, a long line loomed ahead of me.

At last my turn came. I forked over my money and watched the man plunge his arm into a keg of ice and come up waving a dripping bottle. In one fell swoop he wiped it on a towel tied to his belt, popped off the metal cap, and handed me my first Coca-Cola.

Pushing away an image of pagan babies, I tipped the cold bottle to my mouth and gulped ravenously. I paused to breathe; my eyes crossed and filled with hot tears. I blinked them open, took another swig, and another. A million bubbles fizzed, boiled over, burst in the cauldron of my innards. An unexpected belch brought a fiery explosion into my chest, throat, nose, eyes.

Oh, the sting of it! This was like nothing I'd ever tasted.

I'd heard that if you dropped a nail into a bottle of Coca-Cola the nail would soon dissolve. I guess that meant the drink was poison. But they couldn't sell poison. And I'd seen pictures of Santa Claus drinking Coca-Cola, so, undaunted, I drained my bottle.

Coca-Cola became my soda of choice.

Many years passed. The *new and improved* age of advertising dawned and, out of the blue, the Coca-Cola company announced it would retire their ninety-nine-year-old secret formula. They would replace it with a smoother, sweeter drink: New Coke.

They had toyed with their customers' loyalty before. Years earlier, they had started calling the drink simply Coke, and despite the claim that the recipe hadn't changed, connoisseurs detected that the taste had undergone subtle changes from then on. Maybe it was the packaging, the aluminum cans and plastic containers, but Coke didn't have that old pizzazz. And Diet Coke, with artificial sweetener, with or without caffeine, was something else altogether. The same went for Cherry Coke, which should not come bottled at all; it should be concocted at a soda fountain from sickeningly sweet syrup.

I tried New Coke and found it stripped of the one thing that had made *The Pause That Refreshes* different from other sodas; that distinctive bite that had once almost curled my hair. But for me, and many consumers, the original drink was more than a taste; it was a memory. A memory one could still conjure if the newer products were poured into ice-filled glasses and the packaging discarded. This time the company had gone too far; they had tampered with memories.

We raised a ruckus; told them we didn't like New Coke. They admitted they'd made a mistake, and said in addition to the new cola they would bring back the original and call it Coca-Cola Classic.

It was confusing. Now we had Coke, Diet or non-diet, with or without caffeine, cherry flavor, diet or non-diet, with or without caffeine, Tab (their original diet cola), New Coke, and Coca-Cola Classic.

I smelled a rat, in the form of an advertising blitz. Had this been a well-planned strategy in the cola war with Pepsi? A way to introduce a new product and focus media attention on it?

Where would it end? It's like endless sequels to bad movies.

No matter. Call it what they will, Coca-Cola has long been, for me, a taste found only in memory. It comes in frigid, dripping wet, heavy green glass bottles with its name printed on the side in bas-relief script. The five-cent, six-and-a half-ounce bottle has a metal cap that has to be removed with an opener. Every sip bites and stings deliciously. It's the drink I had on the playground in Iowa in the 1940s; the first and only time that Coca-Cola was *The Real Thing*.

It's Good For You

*A spoonful of sugar makes the medicine go
down, in a most delightful way.*

~ ~ Richard M. Sherman and Robert B. Sherman

Cod liver oil.

The words make me cringe as they did in childhood. Those who are familiar with this elixir know what I mean. For those lucky enough to have escaped cod liver oil, get down on your knees and give thanks.

The product is what the name implies; it's oil extracted from the liver of codfish, rich in vitamins A and D. Mothers believed that a daily dose warded off, cured, or lessened the severity of flu, colds, colic, coughs, croup, headaches, warts, boils, piles, mumps, styes, scarlet fever, measles, chicken pox, whooping cough, dandruff, head lice, bedwetting, heartburn, growing pains, polio, constipation (or the reverse), or anything else that ailed you.

"It's good for you," Ma claimed as she poured the liquefied fish into a spoon. We kids scattered in all directions.

"You can take sugar with it," Ma promised, trying to persuade us to come out of the locked bathroom.

"It's the smell that's so bad, not the taste," she tried as Poppy pulled one of us feet first from under the bed. "You won't taste it if you hold your nose."

Lies, lies, lies. Nothing disguised the taste. Think of the vilest thing you have ever tasted. Cod liver oil is a zillion times worse.

We tried this ploy: "There's no use making me take it; I'll throw it up."

Ma replied, "I'll give you another dose until you keep it down."

It was better to take it once and be done with it. It didn't help to gulp the oil down fast—well, you really couldn't. The goop coated your tongue, teeth and throat like a layer of glue and the taste and odor lingered all day.

I have a hazy memory of standing in line in grade school to take a spoonful of cod liver oil. I must have dreamed it; I can't believe they could have made children do that—lambs to the slaughter, so to speak. I need verification from someone who remembers that this actually happened.

Imagine teachers saying, "Boys and girls, right after the Pledge of Allegiance the school nurse will give us our cod liver oil so we'll stay healthy."

They would have had a mutiny on their hands, even in those days when children were seen more often than heard.

I recently checked the shelves at the pharmacy. Cod liver oil now comes in mint flavor. Mint flavor? Who do they think they're kidding?

The bottle has a warning: Keep this preparation away from children.

Sure—now when it's too late for me.

Time marches on; I now take daily fish oil capsules. They're tasteless. Really, they are. They're good for you.

Radio—A Good Neighbor

Good morning, breakfast clubbers, it's time to sing you, another cheery greeting, so now we bring you—first call to breakfast.

~ ~ Don McNeill

Reveille, every school day at eight a.m., came via Don McNeill on his popular program *The Breakfast Club*.

Ma turned up the radio full blast and opened the door to the upstairs. If we slept through the first, second, and third calls and heard, "Last call to breakfast," we had fifteen minutes to dress, grab a handful of Puffed Wheat from the two-foot long package, and race two blocks to school. Larry was always last out the door. I'm sure he holds the school record for being late.

The Breakfast Club, from Chicago, was aired nationwide and into Canada by NBC Blue Network from 1933-1968 (also on television). It was the longest running network entertainment program in history and was inducted into the Radio Hall of Fame in 1989. Big, handsome, and charming, McNeill was aided and abetted by the gossipy Aunt Fanny (Fran Allison) and Grandpa Putterball (Sid Ellstrom). Recorded before an audience, the show featured jokes, stories, music, and surprises, such as celebrities stopping by for a chat, among them Norman Rockwell, Bob Hope, Jimmy Stewart, and Danny Kaye.

Every fifteen minutes, McNeill interrupted with "Let's all march around the breakfast table." He, the cast, the audience, the guests, and folks across the country did just that. The program ended with a hymn and a silent prayer, led by McNeill. "Let's bow our heads in prayer. Each in his own words, each in his own way."

McNeill signed off with, "Don't forget Don McNeill and his gang saying so long and be good to your neighbor."

He died in 1996 at age 88. I still recall the booming voice that woke me five days a week when I was a child.

Another voice that stressed being a good neighbor was that of Wynn Speece. Several years ago, while listening to National Public Radio's *All Things Considered*, I heard a woman reading a recipe and knew at once it was *Your Neighbor Lady*. The occasion was her 60th anniversary of broadcasting from Yankton, South Dakota's WNAX 570, The Great Station of the Great Plains.

Although the show was called *Your Neighbor Lady*, Speece was usually referred to as The Neighbor Lady. She began dispensing household hints and recipes in 1941, before the term "stay-at-home mother" was coined. That's where most mothers were, at home, tuned into their radios while working. On July 14, scores of women across America's north-central prairie found a new companion, a confidante, and a neighbor in Wynn Hubler (later Speece). Her greeting, "Hello there, good friends," reached ten states and Saskatchewan.

For women isolated in the country or in small towns, The Neighbor Lady offered a connection to the world. Proof came in truckloads of letters.

Mrs. H. J. Larson, Sturgis, South Dakota, wrote, "You're the only neighbor I can visit with each day, for out here on the western prairie, people live much farther apart. Sunday is the only visiting day. Now, since gas rationing, there's little visiting. You can understand how glad I am when your visit comes each day."

Those in households without electricity often saved their radio batteries for favorite programs. Women chose The Neighbor Lady over the polka music of a young WNAX accordionist, Lawrence Welk. Alma Davis, Wessington Springs, South Dakota, wrote, "I never realized how much I would miss your program until the radio battery ran down." One woman wrote that her husband conveniently managed to take his coffee break when the program was on. Future homemakers heeded The Neighbor Lady's advice, too. Esther Enders, Winner, South Dakota, wrote that her young daughter explained to her brother how to set the table, "The way The Neighbor Lady told us."

Winifred Hubler was born in 1917 in Marshalltown, Iowa. At Drake University, she wanted to major in Home Economics but Drake did not offer that program, nor her second choice, a radio major (wary of this passing fancy they didn't want students pursuing hopeless futures). Hubler opted for drama and minored in broadcasting. After several disappointing auditions for soap operas in Chicago, she returned to Des Moines and landed a role on a WHO Radio soap. Also beginning a career there was a young sport's announcer: Ronald "Dutch" Reagan.

In 1939, Hubler accepted a job at Yankton's WNAX as a $20 a week continuity writer. Later, she had a fifteen minute Sunday morning program called *Ways To Win With Wynn Hubler*, offering premiums from advertisers. That did so well that she was given another fifteen minute, six days a week program directed at housewives. The title, *Your Neighbor Lady*, came because of Hubler's bit role on the station's western soap opera, where she was referred to as the main character's neighbor lady. Although single and only twenty-three, housewives accepted her because she made them feel their work had value.

When Hubler became engaged to Naval aviator Harry Speece she kept it a secret. Returning from her honeymoon in 1945, she revealed the news on air by calling herself Mrs. Neighbor Lady. Beatrice Lovick, Wallace, South Dakota, wrote, "My Dear Mrs. Neighbor Lady: I want to congratulate you on your marriage. You seem a little more like one of us."

Now a war bride, Mrs. Neighbor Lady identified with women whose husbands were away. Harry Speece became known as HH (husband Harry). With Speece's first pregnancy in 1947, she began broadcasting from home. Over the years, fans celebrated the births of three Speece children and the addition of a teenaged foster daughter. Now their radio friend was a housewife and mother, practicing what she preached. Listeners were amused when one of the children disrupted the broadcast.

The program was a vehicle through which women shared love and concern for family, friends, and strangers. Speece read notes from listeners in which they asked for prayers or cards for someone who was ill or in need. Women responded by forming prayer circles and sending cards and gifts to those mentioned.

By the late 1960s, clutter of other stations meant that WNAX reached only parts of South and North Dakota, Iowa, Nebraska, and Minnesota. In 1973, with radio having lost much of its audience to television, and the women's movement convincing housewives that they would find more satisfaction outside the home, Speece decided to end her thirty-two year old program. She was barely off radio before she was on again. As Marketing Officer for First Dakota National Bank, one of her public relations ideas was an interview program called *Market Basket*. In 1984, WNAX officials asked Speece to reprise *Your Neighbor Lady*. She said, "I never ceased being *Your Neighbor Lady*, in spirit at least."

The annual *Your Neighbor Lady* booklet gave women a chance to contribute recipes, quotations, household hints, and pictures of themselves and their families. Letter excerpts were included: "We are three generations listening to *Your Neighbor Lady*. I have memories of listening to you over a cup of coffee with my mother, as my little girl and I are doing now."

Each issue of the book opened with pictures of the Speece family, but recipes were its heart and soul. Those vintage books, which originally sold for thirty-five cents to a dollar, now bring as much as a hundred dollars at auctions.

Speece said, "The recipe books are an important record of those special years. We printed a thousand the first and second years, then five thousand and finally twenty thousand."

The content and pictures within the books are a nostalgic and historical portrait of the past, with wartime recipes for meatless meals, tips on raising children, conservation ideas, and a fashion parade of clothing from feed sack dresses to miniskirts and hair styles from tightly-permed to elaborately constructed beehives.

In 1999, CNN featured Speece on its Sunday morning show: *Across America With Larry Woods*. Woods learned while researching his subject that she was America's longest-running radio personality. He and his crew spent two weeks filming her routine. Speece commented, "We started at eight in the morning and went to eight at night. I wore 'em out."

While recovering from a heart attack, Speece taped another week of shows from her dining room table. "I'll retire only when I have to," the great-grandmother said. "I'm grateful for all these good years, knowing I was in the right place at the right time."

Speece died in 2007, at age 90. Millions of women throughout the country remember her and agree; she was in the right place at the right time. Her familiar voice coming into their homes was a

God-send. She inspired women to believe that being housewives was important, while at the same time demonstrating that women could balance motherhood and a career.

The Yankton radio station has a Web page on which are posted *Your Neighbor Lady* recipes. That's not as satisfying for me as having her recipe books in hand. My favorite is from 1956, the last one my mother bought before her death a year later. With the cover missing and its coffee stains, it's a tangible memory of coming home from school and finding Ma listening to *Your Neighbor Lady.*

I envision a cold winter day; Ma making doughnuts. She lets me drop the flat "holes" into the bubbling grease. I watch them bob to the surface and turn round and brown. I roll them in sugar and we kids gather around the table and devour the warm pastry.

That's the same table at which we ate breakfast, hurried along by Don McNeill's reminders of how much time we had to get to school.

Larry, that means you, too.

A different version of this story won Third Place in an international *Writer's Digest* competition, and was published in the *Tampa Tribune.* I sent a copy of the newspaper to Wynn Speece, who responded by sending me a copy of a book she'd written with M. Jill Karolevitz: *The Best Of The Neighbor Lady.* She signed it: To Madonna ~~ Thanks for remembering! Fondly, Wynn Speece, Your Neighbor Lady 1998.

Plain And Simple Hearts

To my Valentine:
You tell me others are more fair,
And wittier and wiser, too.
What matters it? I do not care—
Since no one else is you!

Valentine's Day broke the boredom of Iowa's grueling winter. As soon as the showy cards appeared in the window of the Ben Franklin Five-and-Dime, Shirley and I hurried in to make our selections.

Back home, we sorted our cards, choosing the appropriate verse for the teacher and for each classmate. We were careful about the messages on the cards for boys. *Valentine Greetings* was safe, but *Please Be Mine* would give a boy the impression we *liked* him.

When I was in Fifth Grade, I came home from school one day and Ma greeted me with the announcement, "I got a bargain on Valentines. This big package for only a dollar."

That she had chosen our cards was bad enough, but when I saw them I knew Valentine's Day was ruined. The cards had no lacy frills, no lollipops stuck in slots, no crinkly hearts that unfolded when you opened the card, no Cupids aiming arrows. There were no messages such as: *My love is great, my heart is true, and both I offer now to you.* The bargain package held plain construction paper hearts, maybe a hundred of them, each about three inches in diameter.

"They're simple, but pretty," Ma offered.

I knew enough not to voice my thought: Yeah, *simply* awful and *pretty* dreadful. Economy came first at our house.

I pouted as Valentine's Day neared. Ma rounded up some white paper doilies and suggested pasting the red hearts in the center, or adding pictures of flowers or birds cut from magazines. I wrinkled my nose. That would make them look even more homemade. Reluctantly, I addressed the hearts and laid them aside. The next morning I sulked off to school and deposited my pitiful offerings in the decorated box by the window.

For the holiday party, Miss Klein brought heart-shaped cookies and we had chocolate milk instead of white. When Miss Klein asked who would like to be postmen (one girl and one boy), I didn't raise my hand. I didn't want to deliver my lowly declarations of friendship. Then I worried that, because the hearts were small and had no envelopes, they might have fallen to the bottom of the box and would go unnoticed by the postmen. It would be awful if that happened and the kids thought I hadn't brought Valentines.

Not to worry, the plain red hearts showed up among the fancy cards accumulating on desks. Chatter filled the room as children read verses aloud and teased one another about boyfriends and girlfriends or secret pals.

I glanced at the cards I'd received, but I would wait until I got home to read the verses. Shirley and I always played Valentine store; we gathered the cards we all had gotten in school, displayed them on the table and pretended to purchase them.

When the dismissal bell rang, I headed for the cloak room to get my coat. A red-haired, freckled-faced boy stopped me and said, "Your Valentine was the best one I got."

Taken by surprise, I wondered if he had sensed my feelings about the plain red hearts and was only being polite. Or, did he *like* me?

I hurried home, eager to read my cards and see what the message on my Valentine from Fred would reveal.

The Merry Month Of May

God bless the master of this house;
God bless the mistress too,
And all the little children
That round the table go

And now I've sung my short little song;
I must no longer stay.
God bless you all, both great and small
And wish you a happy May Day.

~ ~ Flora Thompson, *The Cottisford Song,*
circa 1880

Mother Nature controls when the rites of spring commence in Iowa. May was a safer bet for festivities than March, when the calendar heralded spring's arrival but there might be freezing temperatures or another blizzard.

Our activity began with May Basket Day, the first day of the month. Children created these gifts for friends from whatever was at hand: Paper doilies, construction paper, Dixie cups, or cottage cheese containers. At my house we used paper napkins (inexpensive). Into the center of an opened square we placed a folded napkin, for strength, and then piled in candy, popcorn, and salted redskin peanuts. The napkin corners were brought together and tied with fabric scraps or ribbon, to which a To-and-From tag was attached.

When delivering baskets, the idea was to place the gift at the door, ring the doorbell and then run before the recipient could catch you. How fast did you run? Like a turtle if you wanted to be kissed by a certain person of the opposite sex; like a gazelle if you wanted to avoid a kiss. What I can't recall is how we ever found anyone home. We were all dashing about making deliveries; we must have run into each.

Many of our friends were neighbors, but for those farther away Poppy drove us on our rounds. One time my cousin Bonnie delivered a basket to me while we were eating supper. She came inside, but I couldn't get up fast enough to chase her. Instead, she slipped around the table and planted a kiss on me.

I harbor a fear that some major company will rediscover May Basket Day and mar its simplicity with commercial baskets, cards, and trinkets. To ward off that calamity, please do not share this article with anyone who might be in cahoots with such a manufacturer. Think Hallmark.

The second Sunday in May is Mother's Day, one day a year allotted to honor our mothers. In my youth, Catholics devoted the entire month to our heavenly Mother, The Blessed Virgin Mary. At home, we created a shrine, complete with a statue of Mary, a vigil candle, and fresh or plastic flowers. We were supposed to daily kneel at the shrine and say the rosary. I probably didn't do that.

Our church held its Crowning of the May Queen (Mary) on Mother's Day afternoon. All school age children were required to participate. If you failed to show up, without good reason, you were doomed to hell, so said the nuns. This fiery punishment also awaited children who refused to serve Mass or sing in choir.

Fashion rules of that era dictated that white clothing be worn only between Decoration Day (Memorial Day) and Labor Day.

But a higher power was wardrobe chairman for this occasion. White was not only accepted, it was preferred. First Communion whites were resurrected and, as females were required to cover their heads in church, the veil was perfect. We also used lace handkerchiefs, large hair bows, or bands of flowers across the head. If an entire white ensemble was impossible, girls wore white blouses and dark skirts; boys wore white shirts, ties, and Sunday trousers. For my twin brothers' first participation, they wore dark trousers, white shirts, black bow ties, and white jackets made from Navy uniforms. They looked like a pair of undersized train porters. Mothers raved about how adorable the twins looked. When they outgrew the jackets, Ma loaned them to friends for their boys. Pastels were acceptable colors. High school Junior and Senior girls who had attended a prom or had perhaps been in a wedding, wore their formals.

A girl from the senior class was chosen to crown Mary as our queen. This girl was also called the May Queen. I don't know how she was selected; perhaps the nuns decided who was most worthy. I never made it. Oh, well; I'd have been too shy anyway for that kind of attention.

The statue of Mary that normally stood on a side altar was moved front and center, just inside the Communion rail. We children paraded up the aisle singing hymns and clutching bundles of flowers to deposit at Mary's feet. These were whatever was blooming at the time, perhaps lilac, spirea, fruit blossoms, and peonies. After placing our bouquets, we flowed like angels into the front pews.

While Mary stood knee deep in flowers, we began another hymn. The May Queen walked up the aisle like a bride, carrying a crown of flowers on a white pillow. She stepped beyond the Communion rail (normally girls were not allowed), genuflected to Mary, and then gingerly climbed a stepstool and placed the crown on Mary's head. At that moment, under Sister's choir director timing, we reached the appropriate line in our hymn: *Oh, Mary, we crown thee with blossoms today. Queen of the angels, queen of the May.*

The May Queen led the congregation in praying the rosary, after which Father Berger spoke about our heavenly mother and her surrogates among us. Then we paraded out into the sunshine, where we tugged off veils and ties. It was a lovely and satisfying ceremony, even if it totally eclipsed Mother's Day. I assume that Catholic mothers did not mind being usurped.

Next up was Poppy Day, on the Saturday before Decoration Day. Children of military veterans were expected to volunteer time selling paper poppies in memory of those who gave their lives in war. We hawked our flowers door-to-door, but prime selling sites were outside taverns. We reasoned that if a guy had money for beer or a game of pool, he'd feel foolish not buying a poppy from a kid.

Decoration Day was May 30th, period. Holidays did not float around to ensure three-day weekends. The day's events included a parade through downtown, speeches, a trip to the cemetery to decorate graves, and family picnics in the park.

However, a few days before Decoration Day was May's most important event: The end of the school term. On the last day, only until noon, we cleaned out our desks and washed the tops. Teacher's pet erased and washed the blackboard and got to hang out the window and clap the erasers free of dust. At the class picnic in the park, we passed around autograph books to be signed. The teacher handed out the dreaded final report card—dreaded until we saw that we'd passed. Then we cheered and ran headlong into three glorious months of summer vacation.

May Queen Day, circa 1947, back left to right,
Shirley, Madonna, front, Larry, Danny

A Good Day For A Hanging

Family love is messy, clinging, and of an annoying and repetitive pattern, like bad wallpaper.

~ ~ P. J. O'Rourke

As summer waned, and the WNAX weatherman Whitey Larson forecast a respite from the energy-sapping heat and humidity, Ma tackled wallpapering.

In anticipation of the day, she had wallpaper on hand, having chosen it after poring over sample books at Walton's Furniture store. The first step involved us kids, enlisted to remove the old paper. We'd start at the top, where winter's dry heat had loosened the paper, and slowly pull, trying to take a strip all the way to the floorboard without a tear. In the dining room, the walls had wainscoting half way up, so the vertical strips were shorter than usual. Ma worked at the stuck paper, wetting the dried paste and scraping with a putty knife.

The next morning at the crack of dawn, it seemed, we awoke to the sound of voices downstairs. Ma had assembled her crew: her sister Goldie and my sister Lorcy. They marched into action, moving furniture, setting up stepladders, chairs, and sawhorses with planks laid across them. They lined up their tools: putty knives, yardsticks, scissors, brushes, and Poppy's metal square. A cauldron of paste bubbled on the stove.

The women rolled out the ceiling paper. Yes, they papered the ceiling in those days. Using the square as a straight edge, Ma tore lengths from the roll and placed one atop the other on the extended kitchen table.

"Why don't you cut it with a scissors?" I asked.

"The edge is more even this way," Ma explained.

Lorcy slapped paste onto the first strip with a wide brush; the other women folded the strip in half, pasted sides together, and lifted it away.

Doing the ceiling looked to be the hardest job. Walking on chairs, ladders, and planks, and hoisting damp eight or ten foot lengths of paper over their heads, the crew laid the paper against the ceiling and smoothed it with handleless brushes pulled from their apron pockets. If the paper went on crooked, they eased it off and began again. And so it went, measuring, tearing, pasting, hanging, and smoothing. The women talked about repeats in the pattern, making sure a cabbage rose had a full bloom.

Shirley and I stayed out of the way, listening to the conversational buzz. It reminded me of a Catechism lesson about people in a tower, babbling in tongues. Sister Cecil said that meant they all spoke a different language but still understood each other.

I wished that were the case here; a lot of what passed between these women was a foreign language. Sometimes, in deference to "little pitchers with big ears," the women lowered their voices or mouthed words, making their sing-song even more difficult to understand.

Aunt Goldie said, "Lily told me that Ruth is pg. She thought she was going through the change, but —"

"Change of life baby," Ma finished.

"H'yeah," Goldie said. She and Ma both used this expression of agreement, more of a sound than a word.

Another woman had female trouble, and someone was married only a month and already showing. Showing what? Showing off that she got married?

"That good-for-nothing man of hers flirts with every woman who comes along." Ma glanced at Lorcy, who was really pretty and had lots of guys flirting with her.

Aunt Goldie added, "He hasn't worked since he got home from the war."

Ma laughed. "He belongs to the Fifty-Two-Twenty Club."

"What's that?" Lorcy asked.

Good; I wondered, too.

"Vets can draw twenty dollars a week unemployment for up to a year. But they're supposed to look for work. He spends his time playing pool and poker. So I hear."

The radio shrieked with static and then kept blaring, one program after another. No one was listening.

Ma started to say something about a woman who was a big bug when a car horn honking in the driveway interrupted. Lorcy glanced out the window. "Be right back," she said and hurried outside.

I knew what big bug meant—a rich person. Or, sometimes, a woman who, without good reason such as money or station in life, put on airs as if she were better than the next person. But I was more interested in what was going on outside. The car's driver dangled his arm out the window and he was holding a cigarette. He put it to Lorcy's mouth and she drew on it and let out the smoke.

"Who is that?" Ma asked me.

"I dunno."

Aunt Goldie butted in. "Say, you know that old maid teacher, the one who teaches typing?"

"H'yeah." Ma brushed damp curls from her eyes.

"They say she's seeing a salesman who comes to town every month and stays at the rooming house where she lives."

"Well, there's a lid for every pot. Maybe she found her match."

What in the world did that mean: a lid for every pot?

"Trouble is," Aunt Goldie said, "he already has a match. He wears a wedding ring."

Ma tsked her disapproval, and the women took a coffee break and sat down on the floor. Scraps of paper clung to their dresses and aprons and to the soles of their shoes. Lorcy came back, but she didn't sit down, probably so they wouldn't smell smoke on her.

Aunt Goldie asked, "Do you think we'll have enough paper?"

"I hope so," Ma said. "I don't want to buy another roll. We'll piece it if we have to. It doesn't have to match in that area behind the buffet that doesn't show."

Then she smiled mischievously, went to the door and called to my little brother, Larry. "I want you to run down to the hardware store and borrow a paper stretcher."

"A what?"

"A paper stretcher. We've run short of paper."

Lorcy laughed. "Tell him he'll find it with the skyhooks and the smooth sandpaper."

Larry started down the street, sore at being taken from play. But not half as sore as when Ma called him back and told him there was no such thing as a paper stretcher, and then having his pals laugh at his being made the fool by a bunch of women.

Shirley and I joined in the women's laughter, pretending we knew all along that there was no such thing as a paper stretcher, and thankful that we hadn't been the butt of the joke.

Guardian Of The Books

A library outranks any one other thing a community can do to benefit its people. It is a never failing spring in the desert.

~~ Andrew Carnegie

When Poppy was house-bound after a heart attack, he sent me to the library to fetch Zane Grey books. He wrote a list of those he'd read and instructed me to bring anything not on the list. It might have been my first time in the library—in any library.

I presented the note to the librarian, Miss Zenobia Walton, and she helped me find the popular Westerns. She showed me the children's section and I chose books for myself. It amazed me that I could leave this wonderful place with my arms full of books; that the librarian trusted me to take care of them and return them on time.

Books that come vividly to mind are a series by Maj Lindman about the adventures of two sets of Swedish triplets: *Flicka, Ricka, and Dicka* are girls; *Snipp, Snapp, and Snurr* are boys. The other favorite is *Geraldine Belinda* by Marguerite Henry. I checked the Internet; my memory of this girl matches the cover illustration. Her dark hair is in long braids; she's wearing a pink dress, a blue coat and blue hat both trimmed with white fur. With her hands tucked into a white fur muff trimmed with blue, and wearing long white stockings and black high-button shoes, she strides forward with a smug facial expression; what today we would call *attitude.*

Her full name is Geraldine Belinda Marybel Scott, sophisticated but selfish. She has twenty-five cents and is headed to the store to spend it all on herself. Returning home and trying to avoid her friends, she loses the playthings she bought. Of course, the other children find her toys and bring them to the door. She invites them in to play. Lesson learned.

Miss Walton was, for that era, the quintessential small town librarian. Presiding from behind a curved desk that divided the single room in half, she stood just tall enough so that her generous bosom rested atop the desk. No matter the season she seemed to be too warm, her plump round face flushed and dotted with perspiration. A spider-webby net veiled her gray hair, pinned into a knot at the back of her head. She wore laced black oxfords with thick heels; her legs were modestly covered by calf-length dresses. I remember flowered prints with white belts, and stiff shantung that whispered when she shuffled about the quiet room.

Speaking aloud was discouraged by Miss Walton's glare or whispered reminder. She closely watched teenagers who came in to study, but instead sat talking and giggling. If one warning did not suffice, she escorted them to the door.

She worked efficiently, using a pencil with a rubber date stamp clipped on the eraser end. She dabbed the dater on an ink pad and then stamped the due date on a slip of paper pasted inside the book. With the pencil, she wrote the call number, the name of the book, and the borrower's name on a card, which she filed in an open slot on her desk. There were no library cards for identification. In this county seat town of twenty-eight hundred, she knew her readers.

Miss Walton seemed to like children. She explained the Dewey Decimal system to them. If a child had no money for the fine on an overdue book, she invented a chore to settle the debt; maybe a walk to the post office to mail a letter or a trip to a grocery store to fetch a couple of boxes for storage. She hung a bulletin board in the foyer on which she encouraged children to display artwork, poetry, or stories. On the opposite wall, a stuffed deer head kept its glassy eyes on the board. Two upright hooves provided a place for men to hang their hat before entering the reading room.

Miss Walton once scolded me for pushing books to the back of the shelves, and made me realign them along the edge. I learned my lesson; today I place my books along the edge of my shelves.

The red brick Carnegie building with a rounded tile roof underwent renovation in the 1980s (maybe another since). The street-level entry on the side of the building is handicapped accessible, and there are now several librarians and a computer section. It's probably called a media center.

When I stopped by after the renovation, the blend of old and new looked nicely done. Still, it was disappointing to see meeting rooms where there were once bookshelves, tables, chairs, magazine racks, a stand on which newspapers skewered with metal rods hung upside down, and a globe that stood on the floor and seemed as huge as the world itself.

Vestiges of the earlier time remained. Downstairs (once a store room), in the children's section, there were tables and chairs that I used as a child. Miss Walton's desk stood unused in a corner. Atop an oak file cabinet lay the stereoscope and double-image postcards that once transported me to exotic lands and entertained me for hours.

Noticeably absent was something that could not be saved and tucked into a corner. My childhood library had a distinctive smell, a compatible blend of old books, book binding paste, newspaper ink, furniture oil, floor wax, that dry, dusty odor steam radiators emit, all of this held together by summer humidity.

When I had visited the library before the addition, that familiar scent immediately enveloped me as I stepped through the French doors. It was so definitive that, had I been blindfolded and led inside, I would have known at once where I was.

That aromatic charm must have escaped out the windows and doors during renovation. There is no trace of it now. Except for what I evoke in memory.

Doggone It

Let sleeping dogs lie.

~ ~ Anonymous

Just beyond Sibley's business district lay a city block square grassy area called The Dog Park. I don't know why; dogs in those days were not taken somewhere to romp with other canines and fetch sticks or balls. Dogs had the run of the town—much to my dismay.

While I'm in awe of the varied animal kingdom throughout the planet, I prefer all creatures great and small in their natural habitat, which is to say not up close and personal with me. I'm going out on a limb here to state that I'm not fond of dogs. I don't fully trust them. I dislike being sniffed, slobbered on, and clawed from feet to waist as the animal climbs my jeans to say hello. I make no apology for these admissions. I have a right to my wariness, as canine lovers do to their admiration and fascination.

Maybe it's because the dogs I encountered as a child did not endear themselves to me. My earliest memory of being frightened by a dog was in Ashton, so I would have been about six. The dog belonged to two bachelors whose last name was Gaster. Their unkempt house and yard seemed to invite kids to conjure tales of ghosts and witches (and whales, but that's another story). If memory serves, their dog was small, but came at passersby with a vengeance, barking and gnashing its teeth and attempting to scale the wrought iron fence. I didn't wait around to see if the beast actually could sprout wings and sail over the fence.

When I was about ten, I made friends with twin girls who were visiting their grandparents down the street. Joyce and Jane lived on a farm and one time they invited me to spend the night, my first sleepover anywhere. Ma stuffed a change of clothes for me into a paper sack and off I went.

On our arrival at the farm, a large animal galloped toward the car.

Did the twins have a pony they'd kept quiet about as a surprise?

No, it was a dog—a gargantuan dog.

This was a dog that, when Mr. Wallrich got out of the car, rose on its hind legs and put its forelegs on the man's shoulders. Mr. Wallrich was about eight feet tall (well, six plus). Come to think of it, his nickname was Speck, but his stature far exceeded what the name implied.

This was a dog that, when I began easing out of the car wanted to greet me in the same manner it had its master.

If this were a dream, I wasn't Elizabeth Taylor in *Lassie Come Home*; I was Fay Wray in *King Kong*.

One of the girls said, "He won't hurt you. He just wants to say hello." Her little brother, Bobby, laughed heinously.

Their mother took pity on me and led the dog away, and the twins and I ran off to investigate the farm. Bobby caught up with us by the pig sty and pretended to shove me over the fence as he said, "Hogs will eat you if you fall in." For a second I thought he said dogs will eat you. Hogs and dogs—this place was dangerous.

After supper the parents went to town for a while. Not to worry, they said, we'll leave the dog in the yard. That satisfied me. We were inside; the dog was outside to handle hoboes who might wander in off the road.

Bobby pestered us from time to time, but we paid little attention until he interrupted our paper doll session by bursting into the room wearing the emperor's new clothes. He danced a jig, took a bow, and then streaked away. I guess, like me, the twins had seen a naked little brother more than once, so we giggled and resumed our game.

The next morning the parents drove us to town for church, and then I was returned home, unscathed but for nightmares about a giant dog.

Not to mention Bobby.

Over the years, we kids had the usual dime store pets: goldfish, small turtles with hand painted backs, and at Easter, fluffy chicks dyed pastel colors. None of these critters lasted more than a week or two (one of my brothers, probably Larry, poured ink in the goldfish bowl). We had a stray kitten for a while, but it either wandered off or had a run-in with a dog. It's too bad the cat didn't stay; we could have used a good mouser in the house.

We had three dogs in the span of a few years: Coco, Coco II, and Pogo. I liked Coco, a fluffy ball of fur, and I wept when he/she was killed by a car. I have no memory of Coco II except that he/she replaced Coco, but I imagine he/she suffered the same fate as the predecessor. They never learned that cars are propelled on roulette wheels.

Dog three, Pogo, a black mutt, was the devil's own. Ma acquired him for the twins, and Dennis was especially attached to him. Pogo preferred human flesh to tires, and he struck fear into the hearts of men who'd survived World War II. If possible, walkers avoided our street. Even a couple of men who usually tottered home inebriated had their wits about them and took a different route. The postman finally told my mother he would not deliver our mail unless the dog was inside. That meant no one on the block would get mail, either. So Pogo became a porch dog until the mail had been delivered.

One day when I came home from work Ma was outside and warned me not to go in through the porch. She said that Pogo had been poisoned and was acting crazy. I peered through the window and saw him thrashing about, throwing himself against the wall.

At one time we would have laid the poison blame on a man who lived across the street, down a couple of houses; a man who kept to himself and who people—well, kids—were convinced lured dogs with tainted bones. But he no longer lived there, so the person responsible could have been any number of folks who'd had enough of Pogo.

It was sad; poisoning is cowardly and the twins loved that perverse mutt. Ma even liked him and scoffed at how others feared him.

The last household pet was Ma's pesky parakeet, Dickie, who should have been named Houdini. He picked the lock on his cage door and had the run of the house. Not long after Ma died, Dickie flew the coop—out an open door.

Years later, when I had a young child, I succumbed to her longing for a dog. It didn't work; I couldn't tolerate the overactive pup. The bereft child had to settle for a guinea pig, and a long line of hamsters, one at a time and all named Gink. In college, she had a rabbit, and then a cat. She gradually added three more cats. While living in South Africa, she and her husband adopted two large dogs. Back in Virginia, their menagerie is down to two cats and one dog.

Once when the family was coming to visit, the oldest child said she couldn't wait to see my pets. What to do? I purchased two fish, which Grace and her younger sister, Sarah, named and fed while they were here. Goldie and Sunny had the usual life expectancy of fish and were not replaced. By the next time the kids visited, they'd forgotten about Granny's pets. Except for thinking the gators in the pond out back were pets. One, we named Snappy.

Living here on Worlud Pond, with a woodland preserve behind it, is like having the Discovery channel on a panoramic screen. There are birds of prey: owls, hawks, eagles, vultures, and osprey, and water birds of all kinds, including a lunatic limpkin that screeches day and night. Sandhill cranes strut their stuff in pairs or quartets, often with fuzzy chicks toddling behind. In and around the pond are gators, turtles, otters, toads, snakes, swamp bunnies, squirrels, raccoons, opossums, the ubiquitous lizards, and a host of frogs that set up a mighty chorus than runs from dusk to beyond midnight and from spring to fall. We've seen a mother bobcat and two kittens, and coyotes have been spotted. We've witnessed a gator take down a large bird or two. A gator has, on occasion, wandered up to someone's front door and we once saw one sitting by our mailbox by the road. Yes; we waited before picking up the mail.

Our first year here, Grace discovered a baby gator in the water. She named it Flower Linnet. As babies are wont to do, Flower had a growth spurt and, at about twelve feet in length, became a nuisance. The gator wranglers arrived to cart her away. Grace still believes that one of the many gators that have come and gone since is Flower, *her gator.*

For obvious reasons, household pets are not allowed to roam, so they are paraded on leashes through the neighborhood. We know most of the dogs by name: the now deceased Moses; the black poodle, Joy; and Penny, a Corgi, who is epileptic but spry enough to bark at cars (only certain cars). There's Cuddles, a white poodle; Dottie, a Boston terrier; twin beagles, a chipper Chihuahua; a sporty spaniel; a pair of cocker spaniels; a dawdling dachshund; two Australian shepherds; and a gorgeous reddish Hungarian *Vizsla* named Quint (the fifth of a litter). This breed was used in falconry in the Middle Ages. Quint is a retired guide dog.

Sophie was with us for a while but she became too much for her owner to handle and departed for a new home. Two Jack Russell terriers, Sally and Betty Boop, moved away, but a Jack Russell/Chihuahua mix has surfaced. There's a yappy miniature schnauzer whose bite is worse than his bark. He leaped up and bit a neighbor on the rear and sent him to the ER. Tally Ho's master, 90-year-old Mr. Augustine, carries a swagger stick, horizontal to his body like a British officer, to ensure control of his pet.

I admire a couple of sleek and elegant greyhounds, adopted as pets after the dogs retired from racing at our local track. But my favorites are a mutt named Teaka and her half-sister, Jenny, a cockapoo, who are shameless flirts and cavort wearing flowered pinafores. Their owner says they like wearing dresses.

Some dog owners have invisible fences. Two well-behaved golden retrievers, Moose and Haley, sit peacefully within their area. In the next yard, an overweight, decrepit German shepherd growls and charges as if he's still a menace.

To me, he is; I don't trust him or invisible fences.

Back To School

Sibley has an elegant High School building with eight rooms. The teachers are all the best that can be had, which makes the schools very thorough. A large number of scholars from other places attend here.

If any boy or girl lives in Osceola County during their school days and grows to manhood or womanhood here without a good common school education, the fault must be charged to the parent or the child and not to lack of opportunity.

~ ~ History of Osceola County, Ia. 1892
by D. A. Perkins

Children today are provided an extensive list of items to bring on the first day of school. Staples, OfficeMax, Target, Wal-Mart, and other stores post these lists at the door, grade by grade for each school. The grocery store I frequent fills bags with school items and encourages customers to purchase a bag for a needy child, including the required backpack every kid totes. Some children are now packing cell phones and iPads.

In my childhood, we had fewer needs, but for a large family like mine, back to school shopping was expensive. To my knowledge, there were no merchants asking others to contribute to the cause, thereby adding money to their coffers.

About a week before school started, Poppy announced at noon dinner that he and Ma were going shopping in Worthington (a nearby bigger town).

"Can I go?" we kids yelled as one.

I don't know what system was used to decide who went, but if Ma stood you on a scrap of crisp pink paper that originated at the butcher shop and came home with meat wrapped in it, and she traced around your feet, you weren't going on the shopping trip. You would, however, have new shoes before the day ended. You could only hope the shoes would be a comfortable fit and a popular style, with the latter being most important.

Time stood still while we waited for the returning car to pull into the driveway. We dashed from all directions to help unload packages and carry them inside. There might be one new dress each for Shirley and me; pants and shirts for the boys, and socks and underwear for everyone.

But clothing wasn't the good stuff. From the bags we pulled tablets of lined paper with movie star photos on the covers, quickly grabbing the one featuring a favorite. There were boxes of crayons, bottles of ink, compasses and protractors for the older kids, and pencil boxes. These were narrow wooden boxes with a top that slid open and shut. Nestled inside, in grooved slots, were two pencils, a plastic pencil sharpener, a rubber eraser, a six inch wooden ruler, a wooden pen holder, and two pen points.

School began the day after Labor Day. At the end of the first day, we lugged home our books, our names penciled inside (books were recycled year to year). After stirring up a batch of flour and water paste, we made protective covers for each book, using plain brown paper cut from grocery bags. If Shirley and I were lucky, Ma might have wallpaper scraps big enough to fashion feminine covers.

After school and on weekends, Shirley and I played school; we were the teachers and our younger brothers were the students. Before long, though, real school and playing school became boring. We moved on to other activities and plodded along, awaiting Christmas vacation, and then Valentine's Day, Easter vacation, and, finally, the last day of school.

Report cards in hand, showing that we'd passed to the next grade, we raced out the door, shouting, "School's out, school's out; Teacher let the monkeys out. No more pencils, no more books; no more teachers' dirty looks."

Off we scrambled once again, helter-skelter into summer fun: playing outside long after dark, picnics, the 4th of July, and the County Fair.

My Fantasy Moment

*With great power must also come great
responsibility.*

~ ~ Spider Man

If I had money to spend, a nickel or dime had plenty of purchase
power, and comic books were in my price range. Historians of
pop culture have labeled the 1930s-1950s the Golden Age of
Comics, with the 1940s its peak. The first comic books, produced
about 1933, were reprints of newspaper comic strips. These
were replaced by original stories, illustrated with pictures, in a
magazine about seven inches by nine with a glossy cover.

Some subjects were popular with boys, some with girls,
while others appealed to both. Boys liked cowboys and Indians,
war, crime, horror, science fiction, Terry And The Pirates,
and superheroes Captain Marvel, Superman, Batman, and
the Green Hornet. Girls fancied Wonder Woman, Nancy and
Sluggo, Little Lulu, fantasy, and romance (the latter two being
pretty much the same thing for our age group). Both genders
might choose Mutt and Jeff, Blondie and Dagwood, Archie and
his pals, Disney characters, *Tarzan of the Apes*, and *Ripley's
Believe It Or Not*, to name a few.

After a comic book had been read several times it lost its
appeal. That's when its owner entered the world of Comic Book

Swapping. Condition was everything; a pristine copy obviously had more value than one that a younger sibling had been reading or the dog had tried to eat for lunch. It might take two or three tattered issues to equal a like-new edition. You had to know the territory.

In my neighborhood, the Kingpins of Comic Book Swapping were two sisters, Ramona and Judy, who lived down the alley. They must have had more comic books than any kid in town, probably more than all the other kids combined, maybe even more than Baxter's Newsstand, which was barely more than a walk-in closet, with only a few shelves devoted to comic books.

The problem with the girls having this private enterprise was that they most likely already had the comic I wanted to swap. My only chance was to get up at dawn, be on Baxter's doorstep when a new shipment arrived, buy a comic book in which the ink wasn't dry, read it right there, and then race down the street to visit the czars. That happened only in my dreams, so I had to be content with the hand I was dealt: dog-eared comic books.

Ramona, the elder, was a year younger than me (but bigger), and Judy was a couple years Ramona's junior. Judy wore a hearing aid and glasses and had an obvious physical and intellectual disability of some sort, but she was no slouch at merchandising. For me, it was a lesson in humility encountering either girl, but they were partners, rendering them more intimidating.

They led me to their realm, an enclosed porch where they stored their inventory in cardboard boxes in an order more complicated than the Dewey Decimal System. I showed them my comic book; they each cast a cursory eye and, in unison, said, "We already have that one."

I waited, knowing their technique was to reconsider. Even if they had it, my comic book would be good enough for them to swap with someone else. Their fingers fluttered over the tops of the boxes until one of them plucked out a magazine—clearly not the cream of the crop. "We'll trade you this one."

With barely a glance, I took the deal, grateful to escape from their den of thieves. Then, it often happened that on the way home I'd discover that I'd already read the comic in my hands. Oh, well, maybe I could swap it with someone who didn't have the collection that Ramona and Judy had—which was any other kid in town.

Decades later, four pristine issues of *True Comics* came into my hands. I began to fantasize that I walk into a comic book swap meet, and there they are—Ramona and Judy. Huddled between boxes, they look like those hoarders we read about and pity. I don't pity these two.

I stroll to their booth and place one of my perfect *True Comics* on the table, the other three copies clearly displayed in my hand. The aged partners study me and don't recognize my face. They examine my offering and then look at each other, their secret language still intact. But I understand; they don't have this vintage edition of *True Comics* and are lusting to get their inky hands on it.

Judy wets her index finger and flips through a box. Ramona rummages in another, and another. Judy makes a selection and shows it to Ramona. Ramona nods, and Judy offers me a glistening *Superman*, his muscled arm ending with a clenched fist aimed at me.

I shake my head and say, "I already have that one."

It's Been A Long, Long Time

Don't sit under the apple tree, with anyone else but me,
Till I come marching home.

~ ~ Sam Stent

When the Japanese attacked the Naval base at Pearl Harbor on December 7, 1941, I was six. I have no recollection of the event that President Roosevelt called, "The date that will live in infamy."

Since our family's move to town, Joe and Vince had been serving in the Civilian Conservation Corp. Now, with war declared, they soon enlisted in the Navy. The farm boys were off on adventures they could never have foreseen. In a letter home, Vince wrote that he now understood why people wanted to go to Hawaii. It was beautiful.

My memories of those years are fragmented. I know we used ration books for meat, gasoline, coffee, sugar, butter, nylon stockings, and shoes. We recycled newspapers, tin cans, rubber, and metal scraps. Small banners appeared in household windows, with a star for each member of the family in the war; a gold star for those killed. Several families my parents knew lost a son. A billboard in The Dog Park listed the names of servicemen and women from the county; those who'd died had a special column, with a gold star by their name. Years later,

I wondered about the Gold Star Mother. Was a mother's grief considered greater than that of a father, a sibling, a spouse?

I heard talk that if someone died in the war the family received an insurance payment. The figure ten-thousand dollars comes to mind now, but I don't know if that is correct. At any rate, it was more money than I or my siblings could comprehend, and we were intrigued with the possibilities of what it would buy. In a game akin to Truth or Dare, we asked one another, "Which would you rather have, Joe and Vince or the money?" No one, of course, dared admit wanting the money. The answer was, always, that we would rather have our brothers than any amount of money—even a million, billion, trillion dollars.

We once asked Ma the question and her disapproving look told us we had better never ask again. She said that no amount of money would make up for losing her sons. Young as we were, I guess we knew that. We had, after all, never chosen the money. At some point we figured out that since our brothers were married, the payment would go to their widows. That ended any speculation on what we might do with a sudden fortune. Happily, my brothers survived the war.

Santa Claus brought Shirley and me Little Army Nurse kits. We did our duty while my brothers played war games. At the Royal Theatre, *The March Of Time* newsreels brought the battles home. I waited impatiently for the movie to begin.

Real life air raid drills thrilled us. We called them blackouts. When the siren sounded everyone turned off all lights; even the streetlights blinked out and cars drove without lights. Wardens patrolled the neighborhoods looking for violations. I didn't realize how little chance there was that a rural town in northwest Iowa would be bombed. There was an airbase in Sioux City, sixty miles away, and on the rare occasion a plane from there thundered overhead, we scanned the sky for a glimpse. I remember the whole family jumping up from the dinner table to go outside and see a plane.

One afternoon, an Army plane crashed on a nearby farm. My brother Daryl recalls, "I was in music class and we heard a tremendous crash. After school we learned the news and raced out to see the wreckage."

In addition to his memory, I resorted to a scrapbook of newspaper clippings from World War II. It tells me that the time was January, 1943; the plane was a two-motor Martin B-26 bomber en route from Florida to Omaha, Nebraska. When trouble erupted, they were instructed to fly to Sioux Falls, South Dakota. Six crew members and one passenger parachuted to safety before the plane crashed and exploded in a field.

My two older sisters worked in Sioux City, in a dry cleaner near the airbase. One time they came home to visit, bringing a drawstring from a pajama, which they'd taken as a souvenir from Jimmy Stewart's laundry. To shore up this memory, I checked Google:

Early in World War II, the U.S. Army established a major training base at Sioux City. The Air Base became one of the prime locations for B-17 heavy bomber basic flight qualification training as well as home to various support and maintenance units. Hollywood actor and Pilot-Captain Jimmy Stewart was posted to Sioux City with his squadron in 1943, where he and his crew completed their B-17 qualification prior to deployment overseas.

Ma and Poppy awaited mail from *the boys*. In a letter to Sybella, Ma expressed concern for Vince, who'd been having a difficult time. He'd been in a base hospital around the time that Norma died. Ma said she believed that Joe would handle things better, that he took things more as they came. She thought it might be harder for Vince because had a wife and daughter back home.

After Norma's death, Joe wrote home from the Naval Training Center at Great Lakes, Illinois. It's interesting to note that in this letter, the tables are turned; the son is concerned about his parents: Dad, who'd had a heart attack, and Mom who'd been tending a sick husband and a dying daughter at the same time and had also taken a job at the locker to help make ends meet.

Dear All:

I got the wire telling me of Toots, but had to work all day so I figured that a letter would reach you as quick as a wire or telegram. I couldn't get a leave again so I guess there's nothing we can do about it. I sure wish I could have been there. How is Dad? I'll come over to D.M. and see him when he gets there. [Vet's Hospital in Des Moines]

Did Toots ask about me after I left? Did she have any pain or not? She sure was a swell little kid and we'll all miss her but we mustn't forget to pray for her. I'll send some money for a Mass when I get paid.

Well I must write to Vince also so will close for now. Tell Mom to rest now for awhile as she's been on the go too much. I'd like to have the kids and everyone write, too. Must close for now. Love to all, Joe

Joe was assigned as a cook on a new transport ship, the General Bundy. In a letter to the folks Vince reported that while his own ship was docked in San Francisco, he saw the Bundy, but his ship didn't stay in port long enough for him to find Joe, whom he hadn't seen for two and a half years. Vince wrote, "So near and yet so far."

Joe, now married, too, wrote to Iris:

I see by Mom's letter that you were worried by the Jap's claim of singeing some of our transports and that you went to church and prayed. It's a good thing someone else prayed because I hope to tell you I prayed. I saw a couple of them go down myself. When we left San Francisco we went to Pearl Harbor and from there to Eneivetok, thence to Vliihi in the Carolina Islands and as we passed Yap and Truk we had some Jap planes come over. We got a few of them and the rest of the yellow birds turned tail and ran. We also had a sub attack but our escort destroyers took care of him in a hurry. From Vliihi we went to Okinawa where our outfit got it. The Jap suicide planes are the real thing, as I saw it happen. We brought Marines back from Iwo Jima and also 300 Jap prisoners which we left at Guam. I got some Jap money, will send it later.

In April of 1945, President Franklin D. Roosevelt died unexpectedly. A couple of weeks later, Germany's Adolf Hitler shot himself. I recall those events; I was nearly ten.

After the war ended, and Joe's ship arrived at the Puget Sound Navy Yards in Bremerton, Washington, he wrote to the folks:

There was a ship came out to meet us when we came in, loaded with burlesque girls, and banners strung fore and aft. We were the first ship in since the Jap's quit, and the first of any ship to come since official V-J Day actual surrender.

The 1940s remain my favorite era for novels, movies, and music: Glenn Miller's orchestra; Sinatra; The Andrews Sisters;

Don't Sit Under The Apple Tree; The White Cliffs Of Dover; We'll Meet Again, I'll Be Seeing You.

My clearest war memory involves a song. My sister-in-law, Iris, lived with us for a while. One day after the war had ended, she received a letter from my brother. "Joe's coming home," she announced after reading the V-Mail.

From the radio came the trumpet of Harry James accompanying Helen Forrest singing, *"Kiss me once, and kiss me twice, and kiss me once again; it's been a long, long, time."*

With a smile that defined her personality, Iris crooned, "It *has* been a long, long time."

Joe and Iris

The Singing Kid

The leader of the band is tired
And his eyes are growing old,
But his blood runs through
My instrument
And his song is in my soul —

~ ~ Written and sung by Dan Fogelberg

My oldest brother, Joe, got his first guitar as a teenager. I don't know how and where he obtained it; he was a struggling farmer's son. Maybe someone gave him the instrument; maybe he earned the money as a farmhand. I don't know, either, why he developed an interest in music. We had four cousins who traveled the country with The Texas Rangerettes, a popular all-girl band. Perhaps they inspired him. At any rate, the boy taught himself to play guitar and in pictures from that era his pride is obvious.

A few years later, photos show a different model guitar; this one bore his signature painted in fancy script on the body, and near the neck, Joe: The Singing Kid. Looking recently at his signature on an old letter, the J reminds me of a guitar, the top part of the letter small and the bottom rounded. It looks as if he designed his signature to fit his interest.

In other photos, little Larry holds the instrument like a bass fiddle, and my teenaged sister, Lorcy, pretends to be strumming.

Everyone wanted to get into the act. My three older sisters harmonized when Joe played, perhaps imagining an audition for Major Bowes Original Amateur Hour. Billie and Dolores sometimes sang at Ashton gatherings. Years later, Billie told her daughter that she was proud to have once sung on stage with Bob Wills and The Texas Playboys.

During World War II, aboard ship during a typhoon, Joe lost The Singing Kid instrument. When he returned to Iowa, he purchased another guitar and had one or more the rest of his life, eventually going acoustical. He played with small groups, making a few bucks, or nothing at all. His wife, Iris, often accompanied him to dances and sometimes sang with the band. This music was called "old-time," and I, a hip teen, thought it was corny. That included anything to do with The Grand Ole Opry. Some years later, "old time music" became fully accepted and popular as "country," leaving me to realize that my brother *was country, when country wasn't cool.*

A local teenager asked Joe to give him lessons. The first session became the last when the student started telling the teacher how to play. When Joe retold the story it came with a laugh and an unspoken but clear message, "The nerve of that kid."

In 1953, Joe splurged on a new guitar. The receipt, bearing his signature and the instrument's serial number, is from the Williams Piano Company in Sioux Falls, South Dakota. He purchased a 1952 Fender Telecaster for $189.50, and an amplifier for $109.50. With his trade-in guitar bringing $50.00, the bill totaled $249.00. That was a lot of money. The receipt shows he made no down payment, and charged it, unusual for that era.

Joe moved his family to Illinois and then Wisconsin, where he played with groups at local functions. Generally modest and shy, he blossomed with a guitar on his lap and provided music at family reunions. Sometimes our brother-in-law, Cy, sat down to the piano and the two men jammed for their captive audience. Before long my two older sisters might sidle up to the mike and, as they had in the 1940s, sing *Sioux City Sioux* and *Don't Fence Me In.*

Joe and the Fender that his daughters dubbed Ol' Joe were silenced in November of 1995. After Joe's death, Ol' Joe became treasured by his wife and four daughters, not for its vintage market value, but because of what it had meant to Joe. He knew it was valuable, but he wouldn't have parted with it for any price. The Fender Telecaster guitar is one of the most popular solid body electric guitars ever made. The Fender Company, on its Web site, says, "One of the longest-running production models in Fender's history, the Telecaster guitar has been modified only slightly in its more than 50 years, legendary years, with its great strength inherent in its classic simplicity."

After Iris died, her daughters faced a decision; keep the instrument for its sentimental value, or sell it? The vote was three to one to sell. After researching prices, and the best way to handle the sale, Ol' Joe left home. Before taking the guitar to the music center that would find a buyer, each daughter placed a note about Dad and their memories of his music inside the case. Theresa wrote this poem:

A Man and his Guitar

His treasure was purchased, before I was born.
His instrument had strings; no it wasn't a horn.
When he held his Fender, he felt like a king;
It was his crown; his Hope Diamond ring.
He played it for years, not reading a note;
He played country classics, and some stuff he wrote.
It was brought to gatherings of family and friends;
He played what he loved, never following trends.

So, when we hear that music, no matter where we are,
We always feel the love, for that man and his guitar.
When he was called to Heaven, to meet his wondrous master,
I'm sure he'd have flown higher, if he'd had his Telecaster.
In Loving Memory of Joe Dries 6/3/22–11/2/95

The women didn't expect to hear another word about the beloved instrument. It was gone. But because of the notes they'd left, the new owner's daughter, Elizabeth, contacted them by e-mail. She wrote, "The words y'all wrote about your father mean a lot to me because I feel the same way about my dad and his guitars."

Marcia, the hold-out on selling, responded, "Thanks for contacting me. I was hoping the guitar went to someone who looks at it as a treasure and not just an investment. I would love to stay in contact with you."

Theresa wrote, "We hoped Dad's guitar would land in the hands of someone who would appreciate it as much as we loved hearing Dad play it."

Elizabeth responded, "My dad does invest in guitars, but he sees each one as a treasure and doesn't plan to sell them. He'd like to open a Fender Museum and tell each guitar's story the best we can. I love the way Ol' Joe is worn; it seems to have a good history. We will love and treasure this beautiful guitar. It means more now that we know it was cherished by your father. We have already had plenty of careful fun with Ol' Joe."

Marcia said later, "There will always be a sad spot in my heart to have to sell it, but maybe someday I'll get to see it again and hear it played."

Joe with first guitar, middle, Merlyn, Norma holding Shirley, front, Sybella, Dolores, Madonna, Gary, Vince, circa 1938

Bully For Me

Schoolboys are a merciless race; individually they are angels, but together, especially in schools, they are often merciless.

~ ~ Fyodor Dostoyevsky, *The Brothers Karamazov*

There is an enormous media focus today on bullying, with scores of Web sites devoted to the problem. A White House Conference On Bullying brought together educators and politicians urging individuals to join the campaign against harassment. Celebrities have chosen bullying as their social cause, sometimes citing examples from childhood.

While I don't condone the cowardly act, and my commentary here is not intended to make light of the problem, there have always been bullies and quite likely always will be. Stand up and be counted if you never made fun of another kid. It's a rite of childhood.

For those inclined to go beyond poking fun at someone, to menacing others, verbally, physically, and electronically, social awareness and laws mean nothing. We can preach and teach our children and teenagers but, again, some will harass others for their clothes, hair, weight, a disability, sexual preference, or for no apparent reason. Tragically, children have committed suicide because they felt bullied. The question arises: Are we overprotecting children today to the point that they have little or no coping skills and resort too quickly to a solution that is irrevocable?

Nor is my recall here of how it was in my youth an attempt to say it was the best way to handle things. It's only a glimpse at the way it was when children pretty much fended for themselves.

If fathers did step in, it was apt to be advice to their sons to fight their battles like a man, and maybe a lesson or two in boxing maneuvers. When Buster came home with a black eye, a bloodied nose, and scraped body parts, Mom wiped the nose with a wet dishtowel and grabbed a hunk of beef steak from the fridge to apply to the eye. She got out the tin of salve, smeared a greasy dab on the scrapes and wrapped them with a clean white cloth, tearing the end into two pieces to tie the bandage into place. When Dad arrived from work, he most likely patted Buster on the head and asked how the other kid had fared.

While boys commonly duked it up on the playground or in alleys, girls took a saner approach—hiding from bullies—when possible.

There was a boy younger than me whose nickname was Tuffy, but I never had cause to fear him. I don't even know if he behaved badly; maybe he just got stuck with a childhood moniker. Shirley's and my nemesis was, collectively, the Sharlepp brothers—one my age and twins Shirley's age. Although they held sway with a reputation of being bad guys, they never actually harmed us. Maybe our fear was mostly imagination. It doesn't matter if what you fear is really *out there*, if you believe that it is.

My only close encounter came one day when I stepped out of Jack Lyon's ice cream shop with a double dip cone (a nickel's worth). Before I enjoyed so much as a lick, the twins approached and one of them, without breaking stride, reached out and grabbed the ice cream off the cone. He walked away slurping the frozen treat from his hands.

Another time, Shirley and I were walking home from town after dark when we spotted the boys. To avoid them, we headed north, out of our way, and ended up hiding in a corner on the nun's house open porch. Would God let harm come to us there? If worse came to worse, we could knock on the door of the darkened house. What better place to ask for asylum?

From our niche, we could see our house, illuminated by the street lights on the boulevard. But the one block distance stretched to a mile in our minds as we discussed our dilemma in a whisper.

"Maybe they didn't even see us."

"Ma is going to wonder where we are."

"What if the nuns come out and find us here?"

"We can't stay here all night."

Eventually, with no sign of the enemy, we decided to run for it.

Hearts pounding, we dashed across the street to the front of Sieman's house and paused. Then we skulked out of the shadows onto the paved road. The gazebo in Sieman's backyard that looked inviting in daylight now loomed as a ghostly apparition. Could the boys be hiding within its screened shelter, waiting to pop out at us?

Were they in the alley we now passed between Sieman's house and Groendyke's?

Maybe across the street in Mauch's darkened yard?

An owl hooted; a dog growled in response.

Were those footsteps behind us, or was the wind bending branches in the towering trees?

Panting, we reached the boulevard and, at last, the safety of our porch. We waited, peering out the windows, watching for the bullies.

Still no sign of them; maybe they hadn't been after us at all. Or they'd found someone else to torment.

We had dodged them this time, but would remain wary and alert.

That's Nunsense

*Be faithful in small things because it is in them
that your strength lies.*

~ ~ Mother Teresa

Many Catholics tell stories about their bad experiences with
nuns. I have none of those tales. I remember the nuns of my
childhood with fondness (and for the safety of their porch) and,
for this story, with a touch of irreverence.

There were usually three nuns assigned to our parish. Sister
Cecil is the one I most remember. With no Catholic school in
town, the nuns held catechism classes on Saturday mornings,
in rooms at the old church a block north of our Ninth Street
house. In those classes we were prepared for First Confession,
First Communion, and Confirmation. The nuns also conducted
choir practice and were in charge of teaching altar boys to serve
Mass and scheduling their service.

Nuns were a curiosity. Were they bald under their headgear?
What kind of underclothes did they wear, and what kind of
nightgowns? Why did they become nuns in the first place?
We knew they had heard "the call," but just what was that?
A summons from God himself? And it was forever; the vows
could not be broken. A nun was married to Christ.

But that wasn't true about it being forever because Poppy's sister, Cecelia, had been a nun. I didn't know her during that time period (I was too young) and as a child I was not privy to the reason for her no longer being a nun. I later learned that she didn't want to enter the convent; that her parents insisted. The reason for her release was medical problems, which my sister explained was a nervous breakdown. Aunt Cel became a teacher, and never married. Maybe that was a stipulation of the release; that she was still married to Christ.

I was inside the nun's house once or twice and it looked pretty much like any other. From the hallway, I saw one nun sitting in the parlor reading, while another, wearing a dark apron over her habit, came from the kitchen to greet me, for whatever reason or errand I'd come calling.

My curiosity about nuns was no match for their awe of the priesthood, second only to their allegiance and respect for the pope. A picture of Pope Pius the Twelfth hung in the classroom above Sister Cecil's desk.

A couple of times a year, during catechism class, Sister announced, "Father Berger might visit us today, so let's review our lessons in case he asks a few questions." *Might* visit us? She knew he was coming. *Might* ask questions? He would.

She quickly drilled us, and then reviewed the protocol for the visit, a choreography that included what to say, when to say it, and the meaning of her head nods and hand signals to us. The performance varied little each time the priest *stopped by.*

Throughout this instruction, Sister watched the door and several times pulled her watch from within the layers of her clothing. We didn't need to watch the door or the clock; we knew when Father appeared by the look on Sister's face.

Her first hand signal meant rise and greet Father.

On our feet, we chanted, "Good morning, Father."

He gave us his avuncular smile and responded, "Good morning boys and girls. Please be seated."

His instruction overruled any signal or nod Sister might give. We seated ourselves, upright, no slouching.

Sister fingered the crucifix that hung at the bottom of the rosary at her waist. With her other hand, she gave Father the lesson we'd reviewed. He asked a few questions from the book, calling on those who bravely raised their hand. Finally he said, "Well, that's very good, Sister. I won't take any more of your time."

Sister Cecil stepped forward, subserviently. "Father, if you have a few more minutes, we'd be honored if you passed out report cards."

His face registered surprise. "Oh, is it report card day?"

That was pretty nearly a lie for a priest. His name was signed at the bottom of our cards and he knew darn well they were due today.

"I'd be happy to hand them out," he said.

We each stood when he called our name and waited while he studied the card and commented: Very good, or, My, my, perfect attendance, or the noncommittal, Umm hmmm.

When that ordeal was finished and we'd thanked him, Father made ready to exit, knowing full well there would be an encore. On a cue from Sister, we rose, and the student who'd been earlier chosen as spokesman, asked, "Father, may we have your blessing?"

We knelt in place while he prayed over us.

On our feet again, we said in unison, "Thank you, Father." And then, at Sister's nod, "Goodbye, Father."

She added her own, "Thank you for coming, Father. Good day."

He smiled, and waved two fingers (like the pope on the wall) and quietly departed.

Sister beamed at us; we hadn't embarrassed her.

"Wasn't it nice of Father to take time from his busy day to visit us?"

Busy? What did he do all day? Said Mass in the morning and then?

"Yes, Sister," we responded.

And class commenced again.

Finders Keepers

Losers weepers.

~ ~ Relates to an ancient Roman law

We kids provided our own entertainment. I don't recall ever playing inside someone's house, nor having a friend play in mine. On a porch, yes, and once in a basement, but never indoors. We simply sauntered into the neighborhood, found a couple of other kids, and decided what to do.

There were boys-only games, girls-only games, and combined play, maybe an early evening game of softball. We girls were always ready to toss a handful of jacks, jump rope, play with dolls, or pretend to be movie stars. Although boys were excluded from our movie star game, we couldn't stop them from gathering around and laughing as we sang and danced our musical extravaganzas on Enright's front steps.

One day I wandered outside, listening for a moment to the mourning doves calling softly from the old barn behind our house. I noticed something lying on the sidewalk, beyond the tiger lily bed. Approaching, I saw a small suitcase with the contents strewn about. They were doll clothes. This did not belong to any of my friends; I'd have seen this enviable collection if it had.

Maybe it had fallen out of a bicycle basket.

I stuffed the clothes into the suitcase and scooted inside before the owner might retrace her route and come looking for her treasure.

Seated at the dining room table, I laid out each garment: dresses, skirts, blouses, pinafores, overalls, nightgowns, pajamas, and knit sweaters. Cute as they were, they were of no use to me. They weren't the right size or shape to fit my doll from Christmas. No matter; I would save the clothes and request a doll to fit them next Christmas.

Then Ma entered the room and asked, "What's all that?" Like me knowing the clothes did not belong to any of my friends, she knew they did not belong to me.

Trying to play down the importance of my find, I scooped everything into a heap and said, "I found it on the sidewalk. Someone must have thrown it away."

Ma inspected the stitching on a flowered dress. "This is handmade, nicely sewn. They weren't thrown away. They belong to someone." Then she lowered the boom. "You can't keep them."

As she left the room, I mumbled, "Finders keepers."

While I continued admiring the garments, there came a knock at the kitchen door. I held my breath. An unfamiliar voice asked Ma, "Did anyone here find a suitcase of doll clothes?"

Maybe it's not this one, I thought. However, I knew it was a remote possibility that two suitcases full of doll clothes had been lost.

"Madonna," Ma called, "someone's here about the clothes."

I plodded to the door. The Kewpie doll in the girl's arms added fuel to my disappointment. I wanted a Kewpie doll and this girl not only had one, she had an entire wardrobe for it.

She said, "My little sister was playing with my doll and she said she left the clothes up this way."

I imagined a scene in which Ma had not seen the clothes and in which my response would have been "Sorry, haven't seen them." But knowing it was a venial sin to lie and a mortal sin to steal, I handed over the goods.

"Thanks," the girl said, and turned to leave. Then she swung around. "Do you want to play dolls?"

Her name was Georgia and she had moved in down the street. Her grandmother had made the clothes.

Living in the same neighborhood, we'd have eventually met without the lost suitcase. But I probably wouldn't remember the circumstances so vividly, nor with so much satisfaction as I do when I look at the genuine Rose O'Neill Kewpie doll I have in my collection today.

Alas, she's naked.

Where's that suitcase of clothes when I need it?

Is It Cold Enough For You

Winter is the season in which people try to keep the house as warm as it was in the summer, when they complained about the heat.

~ ~ Author Unknown

For those unfamiliar with Iowa, the winters are long and sometimes brutal, with snow hip deep on a child, and biting, penetrating wind, icicles as thick as Popeye's muscle, sleet, ice, slush, drizzle, and full-blown blizzards. The air is as thin and sharp as a razor, lacerating through the skin and scarring the bones. Yes, we walked to school in every kind of weather, but in my case two blocks, not a mile, as some folks claim, and not in blizzards. A town whistle informed us if school was closed. Music to our ears, but not to Ma's.

We lived in three houses before moving in 1944 to the Ninth Street house along Sibley's only boulevard. In a letter to Sybella, Ma reported that the house needed lots of work. In my letter to my sister I complained: We got the dumbest room [me, Shirley, Larry, Danny] because we got boxes in our room. The boys [the older three] and Deloris got real nice rooms. I sleep with Deloris sometimes.

Our *room* is better described as a landing at the top of the stairs, with space enough for two or three double beds and a couple of bureaus. All traffic flowed through this area so there was no privacy, not that anyone in our family ever had privacy or even knew the meaning of the word. When Delores later moved to Sioux City, Shirley and I got her private room at the front of the house and the little boys remained on the hall landing.

This house was colder than a barn on a windswept prairie. Despite storm doors and windows and the tarpaper Poppy and the older boys wrapped around the foundation, the rooms were never even close to cozy. Well, maybe in the dining room, where the oil burning stove sat in the corner. Maybe in the parlor, right next to the dining room. My parents' downstairs bedroom was too far from the stove to collect any heat.

The kitchen was warmed by a cook stove that burned dried corn cobs. Bulging from its side, a reservoir provided hot water (if we remembered to fill it). After we got a gas stove, the oven had to be used to take away the chill. Ma turned on the oven in the morning and made toast in the broiler, which held a half dozen or more slices of bread at a time. A toaster that made two at a time had little use at our house. We slathered the crisp (or burned) toast from the broiler with peanut butter, jam, or apple butter.

Off the kitchen, separated by a closed door, was a room we called the shanty, which had no heat. Before we had a refrigerator, our icebox sat in the shanty. A block of ice purchased in the winter lasted a whole lot longer than it did in summer. In fact, we probably didn't need ice in winter; the shanty alone kept perishables from going bad. In summer, Ma did laundry in the shanty; in winter she brought the washing machine into the kitchen.

As for the upstairs bedrooms, the stovepipe on the oil burner ran up into the older boys' dorm, so they had the prime nest. Poppy cut a vent in the parlor ceiling that led to Shirley's and my room. It let a bit of warm air through when it wasn't clogged with dust and lint from our floor, or clothes we'd left on the floor. The door to the upstairs was left open so some of the downstairs air might rise to the sleep area on the landing. But in the main, it was a simple case of supply and demand; the stove didn't generate enough heat for much of it to waft upstairs or anywhere else.

We slept under Ma's homemade quilts and covered our heads, but we were still cold. In the morning, we grabbed our clothes and fled downstairs and huddled around the stove to dress. We had no carpets to protect our feet. Linoleum is frigid in the winter. A half dozen pair of woolen mittens, shrunken and stiff as mummies, had dried atop the oil burner overnight. I recall the odor of wet mittens drying on the stove or on a radiator, but I cannot describe it. If you ever smelled it, you will remember it. Also atop the stove, a teakettle was supposed to puff moisture into the air, and it sometimes did, if someone remembered to keep water in the pot. Often it scorched dry.

The dining room was the hub of activity. Poppy's chair and the radio were in the corner by the double windows. We ate in the dining room on holidays when both the kitchen table and the dining room table were needed. The rest of the time we did homework at the dining room table, played games, worked jigsaw puzzles, spread out the funny papers, and Ma laid her quilts there to work on. Her quilts were not works of art like many today; they were utilitarian, patchwork, with a layer of cotton batting between the top and bottom pieces. We kids helped tie the layers together.

There was little to be done about the chill factor in the house except pray for warm weather. It inevitably came—with a vengeance.

Walk down the street and you'd hear people greet one another with, "Is it hot enough for you?"

"Well, it's not so much the heat; it's the humidity."

And boy was Iowa humid.

Joe and Vince atop barn, the blizzard of 1936-37

Pride And Prejudice

It's when you know you're licked before you begin but you begin anyway and you see it through no matter what. You rarely win, but sometimes you do.

~ ~ Atticus Finch, *To Kill A Mockingbird*,
Harper Lee, 1962

Sibley teemed with a melting pot of ethnic backgrounds: Italian, Irish, Dutch, Scots, English, German, Scandinavian, French, at least one Greek family, and a Polish woman who arrived after the war through the Displaced Persons program. It was not unusual to hear some of these languages spoken on the street or in stores. In the early years of her marriage, Ma felt slighted when her in-laws spoke German in her presence. She thought they did it deliberately, but Germans were reluctant to give up their native tongue. In Ashton, the priest spoke German at Mass well into the 1950s. Old-timers strongly objected when that changed.

During the early 1950s, a Japanese man worked at Priebe's Poultry Processing. I don't know what the reaction to his presence would have been during the war years, but I don't recall it being a problem at this time. What garnered giggles from teenagers was not his being a foreigner, but the innuendo about his job description: chicken sexer. We wondered what that occupation involved. He didn't stay long; maybe his expertise took him from place to place for short periods of time.

Old-country jokes made fun of stingy Scots or the naiveté of Pat and Mike or Ole and Lena. A woman who wasn't stylish, who wore her dresses longer than the current fashion, was described by other women as *Dutchy*. My grandmother laughed at her own heritage when she explained to my sister the difference between Lace Curtain Irish and Shanty Irish, adding that there were also Pigshit Irish. I never learned if she was describing her own family or someone else's.

There were the usual class distinctions: White collar and Blue collar. With a few exceptions (across the tracks and in boxcars), white and blue collar folks resided together, scattered about town. Our neighborhood represented a mix of business owners, a county engineer, a chiropractor, a banker, a variety of blue collar workers, bachelors, spinsters, widows, and the Polish woman earlier mentioned.

As for monetary standards of living, I doubt if anyone in Sibley at that time was *wealthy*, or *rich. Better off* than some might be more accurate, and those assumed to be in that position were doctors and lawyers. My guess is that even they scrambled to make a buck; people did not run to the doctor or lawyer for every little thing.

With secrets hard to keep in a small town, how one behaved might affect standing. Public drunkenness and wife beating, of course, lowered one's reputation. An osteopath's career was ruined by her drinking and her bouts with her drunken common-law spouse. At one time the couple lived across the alley from us. One day Ma found the beaten woman lying by the rhubarb patch. She brought Doc to our house, administered First Aid, and harbored her until she was ready to return to the same situation. She and Ma became friends and Ma now and then went to Doc for treatments.

I'm not sure I ever heard the term *alcoholic* as a kid. People were *drunks* or had *drinking problems.* The demarcation for acceptability seemed to be *where* the indulging occurred. *Drunks* were those who seemed to have no control over the matter and staggered about openly, day or night, from one smoke-filled tavern to the next. Those known to have a *drinking problem* were not so visible; they imbibed at home in their smoke-filled parlor or at The Cedar Cabin, a respectable supper club. During a later time period there was The 9-59 Club and later still, The Country Club. Those with a *drinking problem*, blue and white collar, usually did not make a spectacle of themselves and carried out their jobs with no problem.

In the 1940s, a doctor, known to have a drinking problem, was openly blamed for the death of a child. His parents claimed the doctor made a house call while under the influence and improperly treated the boy. I'm not sure if the case ever went to court, as it would today.

Town teenagers were inclined to fancy themselves a cut above farm kids (hicks), but for the most part it wasn't mean-spirited. Barriers crumbled when kids from both country and town proved themselves through academics, sports, cheerleading, music, drama, debating, and dating.

As for religious bias, there were several Protestant denominations, with probably more discord among the various sects than there was between Protestants and Catholics. Poppy complained about a farmer who came to the vet's office on one pretext or another but then hung around trying to convert Poppy to the Baptist faith. In his wake he left tracts asking: Are you saved? His daughter, my schoolmate, once tried her bully pulpit conversion tactics on me.

One summer folks were a'twitter about a nearby tent revival—Holy Rollers who spoke in tongues while rolling on the ground.

There were no Jewish people in Sibley, to my knowledge, and no Negroes (term used then). All I knew about Jewish people was that Dolores worked for a Jewish man in Sioux City. One year at Christmas she brought home a gift from Mr. Cohen to my mother: a bottle of Mogen David wine. Ma wasn't *a drinker*, but she enjoyed being singled out, and with a laugh she tipped back a small glassful of wine. The gift became a tradition while Delores worked for him.

My only view of Negroes came from a couple of children's books (now banned), and movies, where the actors generally portrayed maids, waiters, or train porters. Or tap danced with Shirley Temple (Bill Bojangles).

This entire preamble about nationality, social class, race, creed, and color began as a lead-in to a story about my mother, and to illustrate that I had limited knowledge about prejudice and bigotry. Dolores once told Ma about a co-worker who commented unfavorably about *a colored woman*. Dolores said that she, feigning innocence, asked the co-worker, "What color was she?" I had to ask Lorcy to explain that.

And lest I canonize my mother for the story that I have now arrived at, I once heard her use the N word (again, fairly common usage back then). I don't know what impact this particular incident had on me at the time. Maybe it's only through hindsight that I see its importance. Nor do I recall exactly when it took place—roughly 1949—and I didn't witness it; I'm recreating Ma's story as best I can.

She was the supper cook at the Palace Café, owned by Johnny Horton, who had moved to Sibley from *down South*. Poppy objected to my mother working, but she enjoyed getting out of the house. Shirley and I were old enough to mind the twins after school and to fix the evening meal, most likely leftovers from noon.

Ma liked her boss and he liked her; she was a steady employee, even working extra hours if he asked. When that happened, Poppy complained, "You might as well be married to John Horton."

One afternoon, Horton somehow got word that a Negro family had gotten off a train that was not scheduled to leave for a couple of hours. They were walking toward town (a couple of blocks) to get something to eat. I believe the family consisted of a man and woman and two children.

There were other cafés in town, and the taverns also served food, but coming from the depot toward the business district, the Palace would be the first dining establishment one would see.

Horton positioned himself at the door. When the family approached, he told them they were not welcome; that he did not serve *Coloreds.*

Diners quickly took note, peering over booths or spinning around on their stools at the counter. Those at the soda fountain had a front row seat.

Ma left the kitchen and went up front to see what was going on. Her boss said that he was taking care of the problem; these folks would not be staying.

Ma told him that if he didn't allow them inside, she was quitting; she would walk out.

He replied that he didn't think she would quit; she needed the job.

She pulled her apron over her head and offered it to him.

He refused the apron, and then said, "I'll send them around to the back door and you can feed them there."

Out of bargaining power, Ma returned to the kitchen, where she served the family plates of food at the back door.

There was no big winner in this negotiation; they all settled for less than they'd wanted—Ma, Horton, and the strangers. Quite likely there was hurt pride all around.

Ma was still huffy about it when she came home, both in the outcome and in Horton. She never felt the same about him.

I don't know how she felt about the fact that she'd taken a stand and then backed down. But if she had walked out, Horton would still not have allowed the family inside, and probably not even at the back door.

I suppose the townsfolk gossiped and shared opinions about this scene for a few days and then it was forgotten. It remains part of our family lore.

The Prince Dined At The Palace

Train Stalled;
Roads Plugged As Fourth Storm Strikes NW
Iowa During Weekend.

~ ~ March 22, 1951,
Sibley Gazette Tribune.

Before that headline ever saw print in our weekly paper everyone in town already knew there was more to the story than a stalled train. My family had gotten the scoop the night it happened, from my mother.

She came home from work later than usual, shucked off her coat, headscarf, and gloves and stood warming her hands over the oil heater in the dining room. She sat down and lifted her feet so the twins could pull off her boots. Rubbing her feet, she said, "There's a train stalled at the depot."

The comment brought only a spark of interest from us kids until she added, "Someone famous was on the train."

Our collective antenna rose. Someone famous? In Sibley? To Shirley and me, ages 13 and 15, respectively, famous meant movie stars. My brothers were more inclined to think of sports figures.

Ma fed us more information. "I cooked supper for him."

Okay, so it was a man, but that didn't narrow the field much.

"Guess who it was," Ma teased.

We tossed around names, while she kept shaking her head. Finally she said, "Henry Fonda."

While we kids gaped at her and began a chorus of questions, Poppy scoffed, "A movie star. No big deal." He often told Shirley and me, when we spent our babysitting money on movie magazines, that actors and actresses were not respectable and should not be idolized. Now, leaning toward the radio, he added, "Pipe down, all of you. I can't hear my program."

Ma motioned us to the parlor, where she explained that the cast of a play called *Mr. Roberts* was on the train, headed for Omaha. The train wouldn't be fixed until morning, so the actors ate at the café and then went to the Garberson Hotel for the night. "Henry Fonda was the only famous one," she said, "but you should've heard people, saying this one or that one was so-and-so."

"Did you get his autograph?" Shirley asked.

"Gosh, I didn't even think of that. Anyway, we were too busy for me to stop. I did carry out the food for his booth while the waitresses were busy. When I put down his plate, I accidentally touched his hand."

"Accidentally on purpose," I said, and we three females laughed.

Ma held out her hand. "Anyone want to touch the hand that touched Henry Fonda?"

Shirley and I did; the boys thought we were silly.

"He's real handsome," Ma continued, "and he seemed nice."

Poppy had appeared in the doorway. "Nice? He's been divorced several times."

"Just once, I think," Ma said.

"More than that."

Shirley and I exchanged raised eyebrows. How did he know so much about Henry Fonda? Had he been secretly reading the magazines he thought we shouldn't buy?

"Anyway," Ma said, "he acted like he was nobody, visiting with folks. Lavonne Woodward interviewed him for the paper."

Poppy yawned, making a loud production of it like he usually did.

"Kids, time for bed. I'm turning in, too. Movie stars might not have to work tomorrow but I do."

In school the next day, dozens of kids who I knew weren't downtown on a school night claimed they'd seen Henry Fonda. Or Loretta Young, Dana Andrews, Bette Davis, Gary Cooper ... To hear them talk, a cast of hundreds had left their footprints on our snowy streets, making us the Midwest's equivalent of Grauman's Chinese Theater. I said nothing, certain that I, through my mother, had come closer to a movie star than any of them.

Before long, a story circulated that Fonda was coming to visit our school, looking for teenagers to be in one of his upcoming movies. Boys came back after noon recess wearing letter sweaters and ties and with their hair freshly greased. Girls had freshened their makeup and hair and donned their prettiest angora sweater sets.

Our English teacher burst all dreams of stardom by reporting that the train had left hours ago. "Mister Fonda, never intended to visit our school," Mrs. Forbes said. "Let's settle down."

In time, the movie star who'd been in our midst became yesterday's news, except at our house. Ma liked to remind us that she had cooked for one of Hollywood's princes. If we complained about having hamburger, again, she'd say, "My hamburgers and fries were good enough for Henry Fonda, and they're good enough for you."

One December Night

Ah, distinctly I remember
it was in the bleak December …

~ ~ Edgar Allan Poe, *The Raven*

Daryl remembers, "I listened to them talk about old times on the farm. I'd never seen Poppy laugh so much. Vince confessed to shenanigans that he and Joe had gotten by with, but Poppy and Ma said they hadn't gotten by with anything. They always knew what their kids were up to."

In December 1952, Merlyn (also known then as Pug) and Daryl were in the Navy. Merlyn was en route home on leave and Daryl was already home. He and Poppy and Ma drove to Hartley, Iowa, to visit Vince and his family.

About half way home (a 30 minute drive), a tire went flat. Daryl wanted to change the tire, but Poppy insisted on doing it alone. When he made up his mind, that was final.

They got in the car, with Daryl in the back. Within minutes, Poppy groaned and slumped over the wheel. Daryl quickly reached over and steered the car into a shallow ditch. Ma knew nothing about cars and he thinks he directed her to put her foot on the brake or turn off the car until he could come around and get in. He pushed Poppy aside as best he could and drove directly to the hospital, with Ma in the back seat.

While Dr. Rizzo was coming from his home down the street, the nurse shook her head at Daryl. After the doctor pronounced Poppy dead, Father Berger came to administer the last rites. It was December 10, 1952, 12:00 a.m.—instant death from a coronary thrombosis.

Daryl called Joe from the hospital and then Daryl and Ma came home and told the rest of us. Father Berger called Vince. Vince said he knew when he heard the priest's voice what the call was about. Joe's wife, Iris, said the same thing; when their phone rang, she told Joe it had to be for him.

Ma later recalled that the hardest part on the way to the hospital was not knowing if Frank was alive or not, although she shook him a couple of times and called his name, with no response.

The funeral was delayed a week to allow Merlyn time to get home, but he didn't make it.

Ma remarked after the service that Frank would have been surprised to see so many people there. He often said that he had no close friends.

Daryl returned to duty and while stationed in Cuba in February 1953, he received a letter from Poppy, postmarked December 2, 1952 (written before Daryl had come home on leave).

Hi Daryl,

Found an old letter of yours yesterday dated 16 Oct. and that is the last one we got. I guess no one has wrote from here either. What are you doing, in last letter you wrote that you might be home middle of Nov. but have not heard from you. Got two letters from Pug last week, he plans on being home for xmas, will leave Eniwetok about now and land at San Diego after 7000 miles.

Had two pheasants for dinner. Gary got them from the butcher at Red Owl. Gary went out a few times but didn't get any. Joe Swartzkoph from Little Rock had a heart attack Sun. and died while hunting. Joe got two pheasants Sunday, Lowell and Barney Reiners didn't get any. They were up from Sioux City Thanksgiving and Sunday. Had four chickens for last Thurs.

Larry has the same sickness now that Gary had a month ago and Dan had it too, kind of a jaundice.

Pug wrote he witnessed an experiment where he was, didn't write much about it, guess you know what he meant, said the island was gone.

Donald and Kate expect to be here around xmas if they can make it. Had a young blizzard here last Tues. and Weds, the roads were bad for a few days. Vince has been busy all fall, still is yet. Goulds sold the café to a Mrs. Peterson. I believe she used to work in creamery. Uncle Lew got a television set, soon will broadcast for Soo City and Soo Falls, so he is all set now. Bud got a swell car, a 1950-4 door eight cylinder, with overdrive, a sportsman green color, only 24,000 miles on it. Mgr. of Council Oak had it.

When do you get a leave, around xmas, let us know. Wahl and Hermann bought a lot to build an office in the spring. It's on a corner where old filling station used to be. How did the Yanks come out, pretty good fight at that. Leroy Lyons said he had a bet coming from you yet on a fight of some kind.

Well, so long, write,

Love from the gang, Dad

The Man With A Grin

A Quarter's Worth Of Love

*Love and fear. Everything the father of a
family says must inspire one or the other.*

~ ~ Unknown

To me, as a child, Poppy seemed tall, imposing, but I later
learned from his military papers that he stood only five-eight.
Nevertheless, he was a man whose authority we didn't question
(if we were wise).

As I matured, I wondered: Who was he, as a person, a man,
a son, a husband, a brother, an uncle, a grandfather, a friend?

Given that all memories are layered with other people's
stories of the way things were, I asked questions, looked at
photos, and read letters Poppy had written. Yes; he was stern
and intimidating, but he had a gentle side, a humorous side, a
loving side, a generous spirit.

I never saw him spank a child, but he once gently kicked
David's butt down the street when he didn't want to go to school.
Oh, wait, he once spanked me. In Ashton, a friend and I were
playing on the porch and we kept ringing the doorbell. Poppy
came out and warned that he would spank the next kid who
did that. He went inside. I rang the bell. He was watching and
opened the door and grabbed me.

One time in Sibley, Merlyn put me on the handlebars of his bike to give me a ride to school. He warned me to keep my feet away from the spokes but, of course, I didn't. We tumbled to the ground. I refused to get back on the bike and ran home crying and took refuge under the table.

Poppy threatened to get down on his hands and knees and pull me out. He'd been sick (his first heart attack) and I guess I understood enough to know that he shouldn't be crawling around on the floor. I scrambled out on my scraped knees and hustled off to school.

Usually, all we needed from Poppy was a look. At night when we wouldn't settle down in bed, he came to the bottom of the stairs and called, "Yip," stretching the word for impact. Our rowdiness ceased. If it began again, he came partway up the stairs and stood in the dark, but said nothing. It was enough to put the fear of Frank into us. We went to sleep.

Poppy called the youngest kids in the family *The Bubs*. In a letter Ma wrote to my sister, she said that Poppy had gone out of town with some other men, to look for work. He didn't want to go because he thought he would miss Danny too much. Danny was then the youngest of ten. After that many children, he could still miss the baby. And he already had a grandchild.

She recalls a grandpa who bought her ice cream; that they walked hand in hand; that he perched her on his lap and combed her curls, with soft gentle hands. She and Danny, sixteen months older, each possessed a head of curls resembling the wood shavings that sprang off Poppy's carpentry plane.

Shirley and I had a natural wave that could be coaxed into curls if Ma twirled strands of hair around her finger and tied each tress into place with rags to be left on overnight. We hated it when Poppy combed our hair. He stood us in front of him while he drew the comb down the middle; the part had to be straight. Then he put bobby pins on each side, but so loose they fell out within minutes.

So that the twins could have the adventure of a train ride, Poppy put them on the train and then drove to the next town to retrieve them. He also took them to our small airport to watch planes take off and land. Dennis remembers one time, on the way to the airport, a young driver on the road somehow dared Poppy to race him, which he did. The twins were only seven when he died, so they have few memories of him. David once said he recalled little more than the jangling of keys hanging from Poppy's belt.

When he had debris to take to the dump, he let us kids go along. He'd comment later to Ma that the darn kids brought home more junk than he took. What did we collect? Maybe a pretty cobalt blue bottle, a roller skate key to replace the one we'd lost, a bed spring to make a pogo stick, a chipped marble, or a movie magazine.

Poppy had a couple of magic tricks he performed for kids, one involving a piece of string, the other a handkerchief and a toothpick (my granddaughter likes that one today).

"Can you do this?" Poppy asked as he patted his head and rubbed his belly at the same time. I couldn't do it, and still can't.

He played the slap hands game with kids. He put one hand on his knee, and then placed a child's hand on top of his. Each person pulled out the bottom hand and placed it on top; and then he went faster and faster until the child couldn't keep up and began giggling.

He played regular checkers, Chinese checkers, and Rummy with us. When Iris lived with us during the war, they played cribbage, with broken matchsticks for pegs.

Priding himself on being good with numbers, he offered to help with arithmetic homework. He used the word *naught* for zero. If I said, "That's not the way the teacher showed us," he insisted that his method was easier and made better sense.

"What does it matter how you get the answer as long as you get it?" he asked.

It mattered to the teacher. She wanted to see the actual computation done her way.

On trips out of town Poppy used math to answer the repetitive question, "When will we be there?"

"If Cherokee is sixty miles away and I drive sixty miles an hour, how long will it take?" he asked.

"Easy," an older kid boasted, wanting to blab the answer. But Poppy directed the question at those who wouldn't know.

Before I began work at J.C. Penney, he used a handful of coins and a few dollar bills to teach me how to make change. No matter that I wouldn't be making change at Penney's; they used pneumatic tubes to send the money to the cashier upstairs.

He further explained an easy way to add and subtract in your head. "If three items each cost ninety-nine cents, all you need to do is think that each is a dollar. That's three dollars, and then you subtract three cents and you have two ninety-seven."

Again, I wouldn't be making change, but the lesson stuck in my head. I probably unconsciously use the method today.

Poppy liked things orderly; a system, he called it. When we kids argued at the table about whose turn it was to wash dishes, he'd tell Ma, "If you had a system, we wouldn't have this commotion; we'd know whose turn it was to do dishes." Ma seemed unconcerned. She knew she wouldn't be doing dishes. Poppy's sister, Cel, talked about her system, too. It must have come from their German upbringing.

German words occasionally popped up. If we butted in with unsolicited comments or advice, he reminded us to not *kibitz*.

If, on a summer evening after supper, we dashed outside and let the screened door slam, he called us back to close it quietly. Even if we were already across the street in Enright's backyard and in position for a game of work-up softball.

Up until the late 1940s, Poppy had an old car, big and bulky with a high body. Daryl thinks it might have been a Dodge from the 1930s. He decided to paint the car green. Right now I'm thinking praying mantis green; a luminescent hue on an exotic insect, but on a big automobile—not so much. Daryl says it's not the green Poppy wanted, that it looked different on the car than it looked in the can, but he couldn't afford to buy another can. It embarrassed me to ride in the colorful monster. Later, he bought a black 1936 Ford, and later still, a maroon 1941 Ford. Both were presentable, in my view.

I don't know if Poppy was what is called a fine-finish carpenter, but he was good enough to work for a construction company after leaving the farm. He kept his tools in a handmade wooden box with a pole for a handle. There were a couple of saws, a square, a drill, a level, screwdrivers, wrenches, pliers, a plane, a couple of hammers, and a folding wooden ruler. The folding ruler fascinated me. I recently bought one at a yard sale, along with one of those flat pencils carpenters carried in a thin, flat overall pocket designed for that purpose.

Poppy didn't mind if we used his tools, but if we didn't put them back in the box and he had to search for them, he cussed us out.

He could cuss in two languages (German and English).

And he had a quick temper. One night in the 1940s, he and Ma were at a dance when a neighbor began telling people to never loan anything to Frank Dries, that he couldn't be trusted to return it. People paid the man no mind because he said the same thing about others. But it riled Poppy, and on the way home he said he was going to get his gun and go back and shoot Bill. When they arrived home, Ma quickly got out of the car and went inside and locked the door. She didn't let Poppy in until he calmed down. Daryl remembers the episode.

Poppy liked listening to radio: Jack Benny, Bob Hope, *The Great Gildersleeve, Edgar Bergen and Charlie McCarthy, Amos and Andy, Lum and Abner,* and *Fibber McGee and Molly,* especially when Fibber opened the hall closet. Three silly popular songs made him laugh out loud: *I'm My Own Grandpa, It's In The Book,* and *Life Gets Tedious, Don't It?*

I don't recall him ever going to a movie like the rest of us did. He read detective and true crime magazines, and Zane Grey westerns.

He rolled his cigarettes, using Prince Albert tobacco. He bought cigarettes only when going on a road trip.

If a man's home is his castle, Poppy's throne was his rocking chair in the dining room. Sometimes he positioned the chair so it was in the way of passersby or children romping. If someone bumped his feet once, he let it pass, but if it happened again, he warned, in a mixture of English and slang German, something like, "*Zsock frratd dumbkof.* Stumble over my big feet again and I'll kick you into the bedroom." He wouldn't, of course, kick us, but we avoided that corner.

Next to his chair, in the smoking cabinet, he had a small metal box (locked) in which he kept papers and other things: a tooth he'd had pulled (the only one he lost) and a souvenir penny from World War II. It was a 1945 Lincoln penny surrounded by a metal frame on which was inscribed: *Victory Day May 8, V-J Day Sept 2,* on one side, and on the other, *There is no substitute for veterinary service.* He said that as long as he had that penny he'd never be broke. I have the penny, and the metal box, but not the tooth.

Poppy faithfully attended Church, but he complained about two things. One; that he had to dress up. He claimed that God didn't care what we wore. Two; that Father Berger was always begging for money. "I wish he'd just give a sermon sometime," he'd say.

Despite complaining, he put his envelope in the collection plate each week, and he also, when a new church was being built, paid for a small stained glass window at the back of the church. I have no idea how much a window like that cost back then, nor where he came up with the money.

He subscribed to two Sunday papers: the *Sioux City Journal* and the *Des Moines Register*. None of us were allowed to read the papers until he had finished them (after Mass and after breakfast). I once fixed his Sunday morning breakfast and he said the eggs were perfect. He liked the two eggs soft, but instead of flipping them over easy, he liked the eggs basted with the grease so a thin layer formed over top.

He took a nap after Sunday dinner. Later, he drove to Breckle's, a small grocery store across from the park. He paid the bill for what we'd charged during the week and bought a ring of bologna and a large tub of cottage cheese, his favorite Sunday night meal, along with canned fruit from Ma's store in the cellar.

Poppy was a Democrat. So was Ma. (In later years, when Danny was berating me for being a Republican, he asked, "Don't you remember how Ma cried when Adlai Stevenson was defeated?" I countered that as adults we're free to make up our own minds about such things. I reminded him that our parents were Catholic, and that he was an atheist.)

Sybella told me that Poppy wanted to be a writer. She recalled seeing a handful of stories he'd written. This might have been during the time he was bedridden after a heart attack. He also tried his hand at drawing. I remember a good facsimile he sketched of the famous World War II pin-up of Betty Grable. It's a back view and she's wearing a white one piece swimsuit, cut almost to the waist in back. Her million dollar legs are shod in spike heels and her blonde hair is upswept in back to form a frothy tiara of ringlets. Hands on her hips, she is glancing over her shoulder, an altogether fetching pose. Look up the photo on the Internet; you'll see.

During the time Poppy was recuperating, Norma was in her last months with us. She also did some writing and drawing; maybe they worked together on this pastime.

After his heart attack, he tended the office of Dr. Wahl and Dr. Hermann. He had knowledge of farm animals, which was mainly what the veterinarian practice was about in a rural area. For work, he wore matching cotton shirts and trousers made by Dickie, gray or dark green. One winter when we all had coughs, he brought cough syrup from the office. After we'd taken a dose, he told us it was for chickens.

While our faces froze with horror, he said, "Chickens cough, haven't you ever heard of croup?"

We'd heard of croup; we had croup.

"Chickens sneeze and have snotty noses just like humans," Poppy added.

"Noses?" someone questioned.

"Well, beaks. It's the same difference. Doc said the medicine won't harm kids."

We tried to prove him wrong by squawking and pretending to lay eggs.

One of Shirley's and my after school jobs was going downtown to get groceries. We took turns; the other one stayed home and helped Ma with chores. Ma made a list, which I took to the office and handed to Poppy. He studied the list and then took his wallet from his shirt pocket. He kept it there because it was safer; someone could steal a wallet from a back pocket, but not the front pocket, buttoned for extra safety. As for the grocery money, it seemed to Shirley and me that if the list was short, he gave us five dollars, and if it was longer, he gave us three bills. Sometimes we had to return for more money, and then return to the store to retrieve the groceries. I'd put the bags in the car for Poppy to bring home. He might give me a nickel and I'd buy an ice cream cone and walk home. If the weather was bad, I'd wait at the office and ride home with Poppy.

While waiting, I flipped through magazines featuring pictures of pig embryos or cow's swollen udders. I read about anthrax, hoof and mouth disease, and hog cholera. I listened to Poppy talk with farmers about coccsidiosis and erysipelas. Mud and manure fell off the farmers' boots and melted on the floor. The office always had an earthy aroma.

I thought Poppy must know everything about animals so I asked him about newts. He laughed and said there was no such thing. I said we had one in school, that it was like a salamander.

"C'mon," he teased, "are you sure it's not a goldfish?"

Like many, maybe even most, families in that era, money was scarce in our household, yet Poppy doled out coins for ice cream, movies, and the county fair. On Kid's Day at the fair, when admission was free from 1:00 p.m. to 6:00, his system allowed us a full afternoon and evening. At one o'clock, he drove us (in the green car) to the fairgrounds, each of us with fifty cents in our pocket and the warning to stay away from the Gypsies. When he finished work at five, he picked us up, took us home for a quick supper and had us back at the fair before they started charging admission.

Gary recalls that we might not have always got what we wanted but we got what we needed. One time it was both.

"I needed a winter jacket and I picked out a dark green suede. Poppy didn't want me to get it because it wasn't heavy enough for winter, and he was right. In the end, it's the one I got and he didn't even make me chip in the five dollars of my own as I had agreed to in the negotiation."

Mike once revived his clearest memory: "One Sunday when I was about fourteen or fifteen, Poppy took me aside to tell me we were having company that afternoon and that if I felt the urge to have a cigarette, I didn't have to slip down the alley. I could light up in the house. That's when I learned that you don't fool your parents as much as you think you do."

He taught one young son, by example, how to be a good neighbor and friend. Danny remembered: "Poppy was planing screens one day when a neighbor came by with a door that needed shaving. When Poppy finished, the man offered money. Poppy shrugged and raised his hands, indicating no. Afterwards, I asked Poppy why he didn't take the money. He said, 'Mr. Brower is a friend of mine.'"

Poppy sent Valentines to his older daughters away from home. One of his letters to Sybella began with: Dear Kidlet, and he closed by drawing a little stick figure and the words: That's my Pop. Sometimes he added phrases from radio programs: *I like to spend each evening with you* (Eddie Cantor), or: *So long everybody, this is Kay Keyser thinking of you.*

He included corny jokes and riddles and gossip. Reporting that a man and woman, who were not married to each other, skipped town together, he added: *Don't know what either had to gain by it. Now if that have been me skipped out with somebody like, oh, for instance, Betty Grable, or Lizzie Honkomp, that would have been something.*

Poppy's compliments came filtered through Ma. One Sunday when I was a teenager, dressed for church in a black blouse and black skirt with a red cinch belt, I noticed Poppy staring at me. Ma later told me that he said I looked good in my outfit.

Businesses stayed open on Saturday nights to accommodate farmers who worked late in the field all week. The townsfolk turned out as well, making Saturday night a social event for all ages, ending with a dance for adults at the Legion Hall. When Shirley and I were young and getting ready for the big night, Poppy would say, "I guess you're going downtown." We'd allow that we were. "I guess you'd like a little spending money," he'd add, and reach in his pocket. We each got a dime and off we went.

One Saturday night when Poppy was distributing dimes, he took me aside and slipped me a quarter. "Don't tell the others," he said.

I don't think he explained the extra money, but I understood. A day or two before I had nearly drowned at the sandpit swimming hole. For Poppy, perhaps unable to articulate his feelings about this near tragedy, the quarter conveyed the message he could not: I'm glad you're safe and sound.

Today I think of it as a quarter's worth of love.

All of these recollections help me know the man we called Poppy; a man I sometimes see in pictures wearing a grin that stretches from ear to ear.

I remember that look from a particular day: November 13, 1945. When I came home from school for noon dinner, Poppy greeted me with a grin and two fingers held up. "Two," he said, "twin boys."

You could have knocked me over with a paper straw. Although babies were common in our household, at age ten I knew nothing about how they arrived there. I hadn't known we were expecting even one.

Back at school, I encountered a classmate telling the teacher that she had a new baby brother.

After the teacher exclaimed over that, I held up two fingers and said, "I have two new brothers, twins."

Anchors On Layaway

Money doesn't grow on trees.

~ ~ Every parent, every era

Although Poppy doled out nickels and dimes for this and that, we kids found ways to earn money. My brothers had paper routes and did chores for neighbors: shoveling snow from walks, mowing lawns, raking leaves, cleaning up after summer storms, or scooping ashes from furnaces and loading in more coal. On the morning after the County Fair carnival left town in the night, the boys arose early and raced to the fairgrounds to search for money lost by attendees and the gypsy carnies. During the war the boys sold scrap iron they'd collected along the railroad tracks or other sites. Gary and his pals had a business enterprise going with the troop trains that stopped at the depot. When the trains arrived, and the troops noticed the nearby creamery, they threw open the windows, money in hand. The boys scrambled back and forth, filling orders for white milk, chocolate milk, buttermilk, and earning generous tips from Uncle Sam's GIs. When the train pulled away, each boy had a pocketful of disposable income.

I suppose girls could have done some of those things, too, but we didn't. At least I didn't.

When I was twelve or thirteen, a neighbor asked if I would be interested in house cleaning for her daughter, who had several young children and was expecting a baby. She would pay twenty-five cents an hour, and it would take three or four hours. Wow; money all my own.

I knew at once what I would buy. Ma's reminder, "Don't count your chickens before they hatch," fell on deaf ears. It wasn't chickens I wanted. It was a jacket I had seen at J.C. Penney—a pea coat.

"Why do you want that coat?" Ma asked. "Why not look around for a pretty one?"

She thought my brothers had looked handsome in their authentic Navy pea coats, and my sister-in-law wore Joe's Navy jacket. Why wasn't the jacket I wanted pretty? It was navy blue, double breasted, with anchors on the buttons, and slash pockets.

For a while, I had coveted Dolores's dark green, belted storm coat with a fake fur collar. She said she'd give it to me when she got tired of it, but she hadn't tired yet and, besides, it would be too big for me.

A pea coat was just the ticket.

On Saturday morning, like Happy the Dwarf, off I went, *Hi Ho, Hi Ho.* I washed and dried breakfast dishes, dusted and polished furniture, made beds, dust mopped under them, and ran a carpet sweeper over the rugs. I'd never seen a carpet sweeper; we didn't have carpet.

When I finished my chores, Mrs. Wick paid me and said she'd see me next Saturday. I went immediately to Penney's, where a clerk helped me pick the right size jacket. I believe the price tag was seven dollars.

"I'd like to put it on layaway," I said, and handed over my money, still warm from clutching it in my fist all the way to the store.

The clerk put my jacket into a box and tied it shut. On a triplicate copy layaway tag, she wrote my name, address, the item, the cost, the amount of my payment and the balance due. She tied one copy to the box, gave me a copy for a receipt, and put the third copy, along with my money, into a cup and pulled a cord. The cup sailed up to the office via pneumatic tube, where the cashier finished the transaction. That was that; they had my money and my coat and I had nothing but a receipt.

Each week when I finished cleaning house, I made a beeline for the store to make a payment. I could have spent some of the money, but that would delay the day when I could claim my jacket. Winter was coming, and this year I would have a fashionable new coat.

Mrs. Wick's baby arrived, and a couple of weeks later when she paid me, she thanked me and said she could manage by herself now. That left me in a bind; even after this payment, there was still a balance due. I don't recall the amount, but it was more than I had any hope of earning in the near future. Jobs for kids my age were few and far between.

Poppy evidentially heard me telling my tale of woe to someone and asked how much I owed. When I told him, he said, "Hmmm."

That wasn't encouraging.

A day or so later, when he came home for dinner he handed me a box. "I paid off your coat," he said.

Did I thank him? I have no idea. I hope so.

In all our family photos there is not one of me wearing that jacket, but I remember it still.

Memory Dolls

In the same way that birds make a nest from nothing, children make a doll of no matter what.

~ ~ Victor Hugo, 19th Century French writer

Years ago, when I began collecting dolls, rescuing nude, bald, and maimed orphans from yard sales and thrift shops, my husband smiled and said, "You must not have had enough dolls when you were a child."

For many families during the Depression, dolls were purchased only at Christmas, if even then. Depending on the doll, they were fairly expensive.

The first doll I'm able to recall came at Christmas when I was maybe four. Through memory's gossamer scrim I see a child holding a doll. It is created from a white stocking, with a ribbon tied around the top to form a head, and the rest of the stocking hanging loose, like the flannel nightgown the child is wearing. The doll has no body or legs underneath the gown. She has yarn hair, and facial features stitched with thread.

Another Christmas, Shirley and I received identical dolls. They had tightly stuffed pink cloth bodies with stiff arms and legs that stuck straight out from the body, making them awkward to cuddle. The backs of the heads were stuffed, and floppy brims attached to mask faces completed the illusion that the dolls were wearing bonnets. They had no hair but for a painted curl on the forehead. What's that rhyme—"There was a little girl, who had a little curl, right in the middle of her forehead. When she was good, she was very good indeed, but when she was bad she was horrid." This doll was by no means horrid, but she wasn't the doll I'd chosen from the Sears catalog. My disappointment must have shown because Ma raved over the dolls and said Santa didn't always have the toys shown in the catalog.

At age six, a playmate, Kathleen DeVries, shared her Penny Dolls with me. These bisque miniatures were available for a penny or two in dime stores. About three inches high, the dolls had solid heads, bodies, and legs, but the spindly arms were movable. Kathleen and I made simple dresses for the dolls. Using a snippet of fabric, we cut tiny armholes and fastened the material in back with a safety pin. Kathleen's mother told us to be careful with the dolls, that they were breakable. I must have wanted to test her warning or felt defiant that day because I deliberately let a doll slip through my fingers onto the sidewalk. It shattered. I was sent home.

One year Santa got it right, again leaving identical dolls for Shirley and me. Made of composition, the arms and legs were jointed. They wore pink dresses and pink bonnets, white underwear and white shoes and stockings. Still no real hair; their curls were painted on their heads, but they were adorable.

Perhaps Shirley and I were hard on dolls and they didn't last long in our care, for by summertime we were in the market for new dolls. We made hollyhock dolls, an old technique that Ma taught us. We picked a blossom and a bud, leaving a stem on the bud. Then we gently poked a hole in the hard part at the top of the blossom and poked the stem into the hole. There we had ballerina dolls to dance across a stage. Their dazzling careers were brief; the blooms quickly wilted, their tutus limp from Iowa's humidity.

I coveted friends' dolls: a Kewpie with a small suitcase of homemade clothes, and a baby doll with curly hair that could be washed. And Ma kept a doll in her cedar chest that was off-limits. It belonged to Norma, who died at age fifteen. The doll now sits in my closet with other dolls.

One summer, Shirley and I discovered a pair of dolls in the Ben Franklin store window. Identical but for hair color (blonde and dark) the composition babies with plump, dimpled, rosy-cheeked faces wore pastel dresses, petticoats adorned with lace ruffles, and white stockings and shoes. Their glassy eyes could open and close, and two pearly teeth sparkled in each heart-shaped mouth. Real curls peeked from beneath their bonnets and hung to their shoulders.

For all their perfection, the dolls were flawed. They were $7.99 each. We did the math, rounding off the figure to $8.00 each and coming up with $16.00 plus tax. A sign suggested a layaway plan for Christmas.

Christmas?

December was light years away. Not only that, with Poppy's worn wallet already stretched to the seams, Shirley and I were not brave enough to approach him about new dolls in July.

Certain that the dolls would soon be sold, we stewed over what to do. "Let's write Poppy a note and ask for them," Shirley suggested.

Together we composed a message. If he would buy the dolls we would be good girls forever. We would not expect new dolls at Christmas. These dolls would be so well-cared for we would never need another. "Let's say we'll give up going to the fair," Shirley said.

Missing the county fair was nearly unthinkable, but we added the P.S. and placed the note in Poppy's "Important

Papers" drawer. Then we waited. Watched. Worried. He didn't look in his drawer every day. What if he didn't find the note for days, or weeks, and someone bought the dolls?

Finally, one evening he opened the drawer. We ducked into the parlor and watched while he unfolded our note. His grin as he passed the paper to Ma was a glimmer of hope, but her sigh after reading the request sapped our optimism.

Poppy called for us. We inched forward, hands joined in solidarity. Sister Cecil had told us in Catechism class about standing before the Lord on Judgment Day, but compared to a summons from Poppy that would be a breeze. He snuffed out a cigarette and then lapsed into a coughing fit that seemed to last a full minute.

I bobbled nervously, lifting one bare foot and then the other off the sticky linoleum. Shirley chewed her lower lip and dug her fingernails into my sweaty palm. Joined as we were, our hearts beat as one.

Poppy's blue eyes bored through his rimless glasses. "You know, don't you, that I can't afford dolls that cost eight bucks apiece."

It was a statement more than a question, but Shirley and I nodded our heads. He slipped the note into his shirt pocket, between an Eversharp mechanical lead pencil, a comb, a folder of cigarette papers, and a can of Prince Albert tobacco. Dismissed, we slunk away.

One day soon after, Poppy came home carrying a bag. He pulled out a box and said, "You'll have to share this. I managed to scrape up enough money for one doll."

Today, I can't dredge even a vague memory of playing with that doll. It didn't survive our childhood and it doesn't appear in family pictures.

Back then, I didn't wonder how Poppy scraped together the money for the doll. I now know that he or Ma probably went without something for themselves to make it possible. And I know that my first doll, the sock doll, was born out of poverty; that there was no money that year for anything store-bought. It was also born out of love and knowledge, for Ma knew that to a little girl, Christmas would be just another day without a doll under the tree. And years later, one summer day, Poppy understood that sometimes young girls simply can't wait for Christmas.

Shirley and Madonna, circa 1946

One Too Many For The Road

Ach du Lieber Himmel

~ ~ German expression meaning:
Oh, for the love of heaven!

Alcoholism has affected several generations of my family. I could blame the Irish: the McLaughlins and the O'Briens, but I lack knowledge of their habits so it would be maternal slander. Likewise, the Dries ancestors. Maybe one great-uncle, but I'll give him the benefit of uncertainty, too. Suffice to say that at least one culprit was my French-Canadian grandfather, Edgar Moore Guertin.

Daryl remembers as a boy encountering Grandpa coming out of a tavern in Ashton. They stopped to talk and Grandpa pulled from his pocket a handful of hard candy (coated with pocket lint). He offered a piece to Daryl, perhaps a bribe that he not tell anyone he'd seen Grandpa. Then he popped a candy in his mouth, an effort to cover his tell-tale breath before heading home to Aggie.

Sybella remembered staying overnight at their house, and hearing Grandpa stumble around in the dark when he came home loaded.

To be clear before I continue, none of us believe that Poppy had a drinking problem. Daryl says that Poppy now and then went downtown of an evening to have a beer. He and his brother,

Bud, might have a beer on Saturday night at Massa's Pool Hall or Tossini's Tavern, which were more respectable establishments than The Barracks. Gary recalls that Uncle Bud sometimes brought a bottle to our house for a special occasion. He says the drink seemed ritualistic, a couple of Germans lifting a glass to toast a holiday or a birthday.

I remember Poppy saying to Ma, "I wouldn't mind stopping for a beer after work, but someone always wants to buy me one and then I'd have to buy him one and then he'll buy another, and so it goes."

That's why what happened one night was out of character for him. I can't pinpoint the exact time of this tale; let's say circa 1950. Daryl recalls the incident; Gary isn't sure he does, and my memory is thin. We've cobbled together our snippets.

Gary thinks Poppy might have gone to a baseball game in which he (Gary) was playing. Poppy ran into a fellow he knew, and after the game they stopped for a beer. Daryl knows the man's name, but we'll not use it here, to protect the possibly innocent. We aren't sure what transpired when the two men got together, but somehow they ended up on the road north. We don't know who was driving nor in whose car. At some point, possibly in the first town north of Sibley, Bigelow, Minnesota, or the next town, Worthington, they were picked up by a lawman and spent the night in jail.

When they were released in the morning, Poppy went directly to work. We had no phone, so he called our neighbor and asked her to tell Maybelle that he would be home at noon.

My parents frequently aired their differences in front of the household. If they'd ever heard of the "Don't argue in front of the children" policy, they didn't heed it. But this time there wasn't really an argument. When we gathered for dinner, Poppy must have already told his story. He sat there quietly, chagrinned, I assume. He had no defense.

Ma, who looked as if she'd been crying, said, "I laid awake all night wondering where you were. Didn't you think I'd be worried? I wonder what people will say." She put food on the table but she didn't eat.

Poppy finished eating and got out his shaving equipment. He shaved after dinner, not in the morning when a passel of kids were scrambling around getting ready for school. About once a week, after shaving, he straddled a chair and called to Ma, "Now the neck." She took the soapy brush and lathered his neck, then took the razor in hand.

Not this day. Poppy always had common sense. In this case: Don't hand a weapon to an angry woman.

None of us recall there being a hearing, or a fine, or any consequence for the men. To inject a note of humor; maybe the scenario is not unlike one where television's Sheriff Andy Taylor put Otis in a cell to sleep it off and then let him go home in the morning.

The Forties And Fifties Merge

A Back Row Seat

*Adding sound to movies would be like putting
lipstick on the Venus de Milo.*

~ ~ Mary Pickford

During the 1940s, the Max family owned the Royal Theatre.
Just before each birthday, kids received in the mail a free pass
to a movie. I later learned that Mrs. Max had collected a list
of names and birthdates from the school. That's how she kept
track of who turned twelve and was no longer eligible for a
child's ticket. The jig was up for lying about your age (not that
I would).

In letters that my older sisters saved, movies are often
mentioned, although we called it *the show*. Ma wrote that the
kids had gone to see *Presenting Lily Mars* and that she and
Toots were going that night. In another letter, Norma (Toots)
hoped to see *Springtime In The Rockies* and *My Gal Sal*, and in
still another I had seen *The Yearling* and thought it was *awful
good*.

By the 1950s, the theatre had been renamed the Max. As
an usher, I earned fifty cents an hour (I think). There were
two aisles, one usher per aisle. On weekends, I saw the same
movie maybe four times, with gaps—like scenes left on the
cutting room floor—while I found a seat for someone. Perks

of the job were free admission to any movie and free popcorn. I never went for popcorn because I wasn't sure the teenager who tended the booth knew who I was and would expect me to hand over a dime. He was the owner's son, and he always seemed cranky.

It seems now that Mr. Max was a one-man employment agency, providing spending money for half the kids in town. I can name a dozen girls who ushered and several guys who were projectionists.

Daryl recalls cleaning the theater on Sunday mornings. "It was quiet and spooky, even with the lights on. My pay was fifty cents and free movies. I could keep any money I found; sometimes a few coins had slipped out of someone's pocket."

The nuns in town frowned on Catholic girls ushering because they might be exposed to movies rated Condemned by the Legion of Decency. Truth be told, from my position in the back, I sometimes viewed as much romance and action from dating couples in darkened corners as there was on screen.

The current owners, Larry and Aileen Pedley, fell in love at the Max. Larry says, "Aileen and I started working there when we were sixteen, in 1963. She was the popcorn girl and I was projectionist. She was so cute and made such good popcorn I asked her to be my bride. We married in 1968, and leased the theatre from Mr. Max. When he died in 1981, we purchased the theatre from his heirs. Our life has revolved around the theatre, including raising three children who took turns cleaning, running the projectors, and making popcorn."

The couples' Website explains the theatre's history.

In 1917, a Mr. Dixon purchased the closed opera house and opened Port's Theatre. Two years later the building was razed and the new auditorium, The Royal Theatre, boasted a lobby, foyer, women's bathroom, its own power supply, 525 seats, and the first air-conditioning in the area.

In 1929, the theatre had new management, Otto Lehman, who installed sound equipment called Talkie Vitaphone. Richard Max moved to Sibley in 1941 and purchased the theatre from Lehman. In 1951, Max designed and installed a new marquee: Max. He introduced one of the first wide screens in the area: Cinemascope. He sold bottles of soda, which had to be consumed in the lobby lest the contents be spilled or the bottles broken in the theatre. Those were the days of double features, so during intermission, movie-goers filled the lobby, enjoying soda pop, a cigarette, and use of the restroom.

Pedley describes the air-conditioning. "It was state of the art for its time and was still in operation into the 70s. On either side of the stage and screen, there were large vertical air vents. Behind the theatre, in a small garage, there was a huge blower with a well near it. In summer, the sliding doors behind the theatre were opened, water was pumped from the well and a fine mist was made over the screen opening. The blower sucked outside air in through the water, cooling it and bringing it into the theatre. Kind of like a Florida Swamp cooler."

Pedley recalls Farmers Day, in conjunction with the John Deere dealer, who held an open house and served hot dogs and pop. "The theatre showed a free movie, with free popcorn and door prizes. It was a big event; unfortunately a lot of farmers wore their work boots to the show and the theatre did not smell the best for a few days."

Pedley writes on his Website:

During the farm crisis we had a hard time getting people to come to a movie. Ticket prices were $3.50 a person. In 1987, we lowered the price to $.99 a ticket. People thought it was neat to hand over a dollar and get change. There was a penny jar and when it was full there was a contest to guess how much money was in the jar. The winner got a year's pass to the theatre. The money went to a local charity. A few years later when sales tax was raised, admission went to $1.00. Not long after that, it was $2.00, due to inflation and the cost of living. Also the movie companies started having a per capita amount, and if that amount wasn't met the movie couldn't be bought.

In 1995, the theatre underwent renovation and expansion. A next door video store was torn down and a new building was put up for a second auditorium. Handicapped accessible restrooms were added and sound equipment was upgraded. The concession stand was enlarged, and new seats and carpet were installed.

Alice Max Krebs contacted Pedley with information about the early years:

In 1942, the theatre was owned by Mrs. Lehman and Ray Isaac. Mr. Lehman had passed away and Mrs. Lehman had no interest in running it. Ray had been a silent partner and did not want to run it, so it was for sale. Dad bought Lehman's half of the business in the summer of 1942 and later bought Ray's share. He also bought the building which I believe both had owned.

The war was on and people couldn't go far from home because gas and tires were rationed but they needed relief from the stressful times, so business was good at the theatre. Tickets for children were 10 cents and for adults 50 cents. Favorite movies were *Abbott* and *Costello*, *Lassie*, and *Bells of St. Mary's*. Popcorn was a nickel, and when candy was available, it was 5 cents a bar. Popcorn business was good during a musical because kids would get bored and needed a drink of water and something to eat.

When I graduated from high school Dad invited the senior class to the show and started a tradition. He would also have a private showing for the nuns and priests in the area for movies that would appeal to them, such as, *The Song of Bernadette* and *Going My Way*.

It's great that you have succeeded in times that must have sometimes been difficult. I wish you continued success.

Pedley adds, "In 2012, we're looking at a different storm cloud. The forecast is for all movie theatres to convert to digital movies and sound. Possibly, as soon as 2013, they will stop making 35mm film. Theatres have the option of converting or closing the door. The cost to convert is around $65,000 per screen. At our age, we ask ourselves whether or not to do this. The sad part is that the 35mm film experience, with its shortcomings of film jerking and scratches, will be gone for future generations. Currently, business is good, depending on the availability of prints. We have two screens showing different movies; we're open nightly and admission for adults is $6.00; children $5.00."

The good news is that—in show biz tradition—the show will go on. Larry Pedley recently informed me: "At this time we are planning on going to digital format. We feel that the presence of a movie theatre in Sibley is too important to let it die. The future is always uncertain, and most likely we will never see a return in the investment, unless you count the faces of those who laughed, cried, or were scared enjoying the magic of movies. We truly believe this and maybe someday we will find new owners who feel the way we do."

I still envision the theatre of the early 1950s: Mrs. Max at the ticket window; her son making popcorn; Mr. Max or Alice taking tickets; MGM musicals, Montgomery Clift, William Holden … and the back row where I stood, flashlight in hand, ready to direct someone to a seat.

The Things We Did Last Summer

*The way to make coaches think you're in shape
in the spring is to get a tan.*

~ ~ Baseball player Whitey Ford

As teenagers, the ideal summer job for my girlfriends and me was anything in the evening: ushering at the theater, babysitting, telephone operator, or car-hopping at a drive-in eatery owned by one friend's parents. Daytime could then be devoted to our top priority: Getting a suntan.

The ritual began on the first warm spring day and continued into fall, weather permitting. We greased ourselves with baby oil laced with iodine. Baby oil cost less than suntan lotion, and the reddish-brown iodine was said to deepen tans. We stretched out on blankets at the sandpit swimming hole or in our backyards and periodically rotated our bodies front to back and back to front, like a turkey on a spit. All summer we compared tans and worried about losing color. When our outer arms got tanner than the inner side, we likened the lighter color to a frog's belly.

After graduating to full-time jobs, we prayed for sunny weekends. Trying to cram seven days exposure into two, we ended up with severe sunburns, and then peeling skin. But at least everyone knew we *were working on a tan.*

Life progresses in odd ways. I had a swimming pool at my last house, around which I could tan privately, and I currently live ten minutes from Siesta Key Beach, ranked as the best beach in America (2011). However—I have more sense than I once had, as well as the knowledge and proof that sunshine damages skin. That news wouldn't have stopped me when I was young and invincible, but as I said, I'm wiser now. I've learned that there are more important things than skin tone. I limit my exposure and use lotions that supposedly filter damaging rays.

I say supposedly because I read recently that studies have shown that these lotions do not effectively block dangerous rays. Another study stated that constant use of sun-block lotions is not good, and that five to fifteen minutes of unprotected exposure to sunshine is beneficial. The sun's vitamin D helps ward off osteoporosis and some types of cancer, lowers cholesterol, boosts energy, enhances memory and concentration, and promotes sound sleep.

Wow; those benefits sound too good to be true.

But what about wrinkles and dry skin?

I don't know what to do.

Maybe I'll go for a walk on the beach and ponder it. The question is: With sun-block or without?

Desperately Seeking Michael Bublé

*Nothing is more singular about a generation
than its addiction to music.*

~ ~ Allan Bloom, Educator

Parents and children have long been at odds about music. The generation chasm probably has roots in the Stone Age, when Junior constructed a set of animal skin drums and pounded away while howling at the moon. "What's that infernal racket?" his mother would have asked.

My mother liked polka bands: The Six Fat Dutchmen, Tiny Hill, and Lawrence Welk, which I thought were corny; as was the old-time music played by my oldest brother's band. Country was not *cool* then. It's likely that no one even imagined it would become as universally popular as it is today, with no generation gap among its listeners. I'm still not a fan.

During my 1950s teen years, Ma poked fun at my favorite group, The Four Freshman, saying they couldn't carry a tune in a bucket. Nor did she like the *be-bop* my older brother favored. Certain that he could prove his music was hip, Mike took Ma to see Stan Kenton. She said the band was just loud noise and that quite likely all the musicians *smoked dope.*

Oy veh; she would have shuddered at the next few generations.

Kenton and other big bands and singing groups appeared at the venerable Roof Garden, a second-story ramshackle pavilion that served as the centerpiece for Arnold's Park Amusement Park at Lake Okoboji. With almost nothing but windows on all sides, lake breezes conditioned the air in the cavernous room.

Built in 1889 (and still operating), the park boasts a roller coaster called The Legend. Erected in 1927, it's the 13th oldest roller coaster in the United States—the first and only roller coaster I ever rode. A friend and her date, and my date, nearly dragged me aboard. In the 1940s, The Legend was the scene of tragedy when the teenaged son of a Sibley dentist, Dr. Parrot, fell from the coaster and died. The story went that he was showing off and stood up in the carriage.

It wasn't the amusements that drew teenagers; it was music. We made the hour's drive in the evening, headed for The Roof Garden, then in its fourth decade. When the mighty bands commenced and the wooden floor filled with energetic dancers, the old building swayed, creaked, rocked, and rolled.

The first celebrity band I heard there was led by Harry James. When I walked into the smoke-filled room and saw, in the spotlight, the handsome man wearing a white jacket and black trousers, the spinning overhead lights bouncing off his golden trumpet, I thought Frank Baum's cyclone had picked me up and then dropped me on a sound stage in Hollywood. I surely wasn't in Iowa anymore.

Ironically, a tornado destroyed The Roof Garden in 1968. By then, it had gone into decline, having hung on through the growth of Rock and Roll and then into the first half of the 1960s. The popular musical acts were big money for promoters and it no longer made financial sense to book them at small venues. There's a new Roof Garden today but it's a different arena, with concerts during the week and rented on weekends for flea markets, trade shows, and company picnics.

An hour's drive from The Lakes stood another music mecca, The Surf Ballroom at Clear Lake. Clear Lake is the site of the February 3, 1959 plane crash that took the lives of Rock and Roll pioneers Buddy Holly, Ritchie Valens, and J.P. "The Big Bopper" Richardson (and pilot Roger Peterson). Another musician, Waylon Jennings, was supposed to have been on the plane but he took a bus instead. The Surf Ballroom was a last minute booking by the group's promoters. Finding themselves with an open date, they called the Surf's manager, who accepted the show. The multiple deaths have since been called the first and greatest tragedy Rock and Roll ever suffered, and The Day The Music Died.

By 1971, when Don McLean wrote and sang his now classic *American Pie* (one of my favorites), the music of my era had disappeared—except for radio stations that played *oldies*. I'd witnessed the Sixties musical revolution of my younger brothers' generation: *American Bandstand*, the Beatles first appearance on *The Ed Sullivan Show*, and the protest and folk songs. I gathered a multitude of enjoyable singers and songs along the way but, gradually, I became lost in the maze. I'm told that Bob Dylan's lyrics were the voice of his generation, but I forgot to send away for the decoder ring that unscrambles his mumble. By the time I knew who The New Kids On The Block were, they were adults; The Back Street Boys could afford a penthouse; and Boyz II Men were grandparents. 'N Snyc? Not me. I thought M&M was everyone's favorite candy. Then I learned that it referred to Eminem, whose foul mouth wins him Grammy awards. *Sigh*.

When I recently asked my nine-year-old granddaughter what music she likes, she told me she only *kind of* likes Justin Bieber. Then she turned on Mom's phone and had me listen to Lady Gaga. I couldn't understand the lyrics but I loved seeing Grace and her sister Sarah groove to the rhythm.

I watch *American Idol* because I enjoy the kids and admire their talent and eagerness. The show harkens back to Ted Mack's *The Original Amateur Hour,* and, during those crazy auditions, to *The Gong Show.* But on *Idol,* unless I know the song (I rarely do), I can't understand the words. No, my hearing is not impaired; I've had it checked. My hearing is probably better than that of much younger people who have listened to loud music all their lives. The problem is—the singers are inarticulate. And when the judges say, "Everyone in America knows this song," I mumble, Nuh uhh.

One 15-year-old contestant angrily screeched and stomped her feet through a fast tempo tune, the content of which I hadn't a clue. I later read that she had sung *Try A Little Tenderness.* Seriously?

My daughter told me that Otis Redding had sung it like she did. Ah; I knew it wasn't Sinatra's romantic version the child had channeled.

Okay, I've come to a conclusion. I'm not saying I'm right, just my opinion. Singers in the 1940s and early 1950s, stood before a mike and sang, enunciating every word, while an orchestra accompanied them, not drowned out the vocal. Music fans who grew up with television are accustomed to and want visuals; a hullabaloo of a stage show with glitter, fireworks, smoke, explosions, costumes, hair styles, cartwheels, confetti, backup singers and dancers, with the upfront singer as ringmaster.

To quote my mother: Just loud noise.

Once when I mentioned that I found today's music unintelligible, a friend (my age) countered with, "The world would be a quiet place if only the birds with the sweetest sounds were allowed to sing."

She's right, of course. But I prefer a meadowlark's trill to a crow's squawk. Give me songs with meaningful lyrics, like this one from the 1950s:

Hey nonny ding dong, alang alang alang
Boom ba-doh, ba-doo ba-doodle-ay.
Sh-boom sh-boom Ya-da-da Da-da-da Da-da-da Da
Sh-boom sh-boom Ya-da-da Da-da-da Da-da-da Da
Sh-boom sh-boom Ya-da-da Da-da-da Da-da-da Da,
sh-boom...

Sh-boom was written by The Chords: James Keyes, Claude Feaster, Carl Feaster, Floyd McRae, and James Edwards. They first recorded the song but the recording by The Crew Cuts became the one we (I) remember.

The Cotton Ball

Carry me back to old Virginny, that's where
the cotton and the corn and taters grow ...

~ ~ James A. Bland

Aging has its blessings; one being gaining the perspective to understand the why and wherefore of situations from the past, and the ability to laugh at what once seemed serious or humiliating. Starting with the lean bones of recall and adding hindsight and humor, I've brewed a fresh story about a night long ago.

At age seventeen, in my last term of high school, I hadn't yet dated (no; that wasn't serious or humiliating). Ma teased me about a couple of homely farm boys who stared at me in church, and she sometimes asked, "What's wrong with (add name here)?" as if the only thing that stood in the way of my going out with someone was that I was too picky. At my age, she'd been courted by a man seven years her senior and married him a year later.

When the Junior-Senior Prom rolled around in May, there wasn't anyone I even suspected might ask to escort me to the big event. But a bee buzzed a message in Ma's bonnet that I should attend the prom, with or without a date. Some kids did go by themselves, forming the stag line and the wallflowers.

Both terms bore the stigma of *can't get a date*. I didn't even like dancing; I felt awkward and inhibited.

It made no difference when I argued that I wasn't going to the dance; Ma proceeded to ask her niece to make my dress. Why didn't I put a stop to the nonsense at that point? Good question.

Maybe because I needed something dressy for the luncheon hosted by the Business and Professional Women for graduating girls. Among the women speaking about career options would be the one female lawyer in town, the librarian, the school nurse, the county welfare director, a teacher, and two women who owned their own business.

So, while at work at Penney's, I chose a pattern for my formal—a rounded scooped neck, capped sleeves, full skirt—and picked the material, pink with a subtle design. One crinoline underneath, and a black narrow grosgrain ribbon circled the waist. Black shoes. White would have looked better for the belt and shoes, but it was considered tacky to wear white before Decoration Day and after Labor Day. Except for men's white shirts, white was reserved for summer.

On Prom day I considered feigning illness. But acting wasn't my *forte*. I didn't have a *forte*.

My carriage and driver arrived in the form of my sister-in-law Iris. Although the dance was held in the school gymnasium, only two blocks away, I'd agreed to be driven because I'd have felt silly strolling down the street in a formal, unescorted. Ma rode along. Prom was not only the social highlight of the school year, it was an outing for women. They lined up to watch the parade of teenagers whose usual garb was Levi's and white bucks and circle skirts and saddle shoes transformed into almost adults in suits and gowns. It was not unlike a Red Carpet extravaganza, but no one interviewed the attendees and asked who they were wearing. If there had been an interview, and if I had been clever enough, I'd have responded, "Design by Butterick; seamstress Cousin Millie."

A rivalry existed about formals, with nothing revealed about them until the big night. Some girls had gone out of town to purchase a gown, as far as Younkers Department Store in Sioux City, or even farther, to Dayton's in Minneapolis. To look their best, and weather permitting, girls had worked on getting a tan, especially the face, torso, and arms. The lily white shoulders of our mothers' day were passé.

I slipped out of the car, smoothed my skirt and hurried inside. The brightly lit lobby revealed a gaggle of boys waiting for their dates who had vanished into the Girl's Room to check their makeup and adjust their hair, the original style all but blown away by the ever-present Iowa wind. Some of the girls had probably gone to Evan's Beauty Shoppe to have their hair cut and styled by Grace. I'd done my own, washed and set in pin curls and dried under the plastic bonnet of my portable hairdryer. I didn't bother with the Girl's Room; I adjusted my hair without benefit of a mirror and entered the gym.

The comparative darkness sheltered me. When my eyes adjusted, I saw that I would enter the dance through an arbor. I'd seen this structure while it was being built by the decorating committee from the junior class, who hosted the prom. The framework of slats had been covered with chicken wire and the holes filled with white facial tissue, puffed into flowers. At the top, a sign read: Welcome To The Cotton Ball.

Ducking through the arbor, I glanced at the seats that were usually filled with sports fans and spotted three dateless classmates. I joined them. (I no longer recall which of my classmates they were.) From the tiered seating, I had a clear view of the full décor for The Cotton Ball.

Keep in mind that my narrative here is with hindsight and that this was 1953, rural Iowa. Like me, quite likely none of the decorating committee had ever been further south than Sioux City. It appeared that what they had in mind was the grandeur of a cotillion at Tara, but on a limited budget. Silvery tinsel streamed from the ceiling, attempting to hide the basketball hoops and darkened score signs. (I wonder now: Were the gray strands intended to replicate Spanish moss dripping from live oaks?)

Along the sides of the room, on what might have been a veranda at the plantation big house, were bistro tables and chairs where a couple could rest and sip a mint julep (er, fruit punch). A couple of tables wrapped in crepe paper served as a bar. Behind it, the chaperones milled about.

The committee members had obviously seen *Show Boat* at the theater a couple of years earlier. Acting as butlers were three or four sophomore boys wearing black pants, white, double-breasted, cropped to the waist jackets with two rows of vertical buttons, and white gloves. And, the boys were in full black face, like a minstrel show. I fully expected one of them to get down on one knee and sing, *You ain't seen nuthin yet.*

I do believe that Sibleyites had not before seen the likes of this prom, nor have they since. (Try for a drawl when you read that sentence.)

A couple on the floor diverted my attention. Navigating his date in a slow dance, the boy wore a white dinner jacket and black trousers. She glided easily with him, wearing a white formal, strapless, considered daring in the 1950s, with a sheer drape across the shoulders. Definitely a Dayton's dress. The pair looked as if they'd stepped off a wedding cake, or off the silver screen at the Max Theater—Sandra Dee and Tab Hunter.

Back to reality. Although I knew the girls beside me, they were not friends of mine. I was friends with a couple of classmates, but the girls I ran around with were two years younger, Shirley's age; some of them neighbors with whom

I'd come of age. So I wasn't particularly comfortable with my fellow wallflowers. I was uncomfortable, period.

Scanning the room, I noted the absence of several female classmates. They obviously hadn't been pushed into attending alone or with friends.

After maybe a half hour, one of the girls beside me suggested a walk downtown to get a Coke. There were free refreshments at the bar on the verandah, but I wasn't keen on crossing the *lawn* to get there. The new P.E. teacher was tending bar. If Miss Sherwood were still here she'd be horrified at the shoes on the gym floor. The floor was sacred; only sneakers or stocking feet allowed. But sports were finished for the year, and the janitors would refinish the floor over the summer.

I didn't like the idea of traipsing downtown in a formal, but if these girls left I'd be alone. Leaving the plantation seemed the best option. Dusk had come, but it wasn't quite dark. Tottering in high heels, two abreast on the sidewalk, our voluminous net dresses and crinolines swaying, we must have looked like a small but clumsy Homecoming float.

Somewhere along the way, a pickup idled alongside us and a boy called, "Where're you pretty girls headed?"

Glad to be on the side away from the road, I shuddered anyway as my walking partner flirted back, "That's for us to know and you to find out."

The vehicle rattled off, blasting a horn that moaned like a wounded animal.

We reached our destination: the Corner Café. The room had only a few patrons, but it wouldn't be long before the movie next door would be over and this place would fill. I wanted to be out of here by that time.

Correction; I wanted out now. Crowded into a booth with our pink, yellow, green, and lavender pastel dresses fluffed around us brought to mind dyed Easter chicks in a basket.

This night couldn't get much worse. At least at the dance the environment had been darkness.

The lavender chick left the roost and sashayed over to the jukebox and slid money into the slot. When Teresa Brewer burst forth with *Till I Waltz Again With You,* and Lavender began moving to the music, dancing with herself, I knew I couldn't get out of here soon enough. And it wasn't only because I couldn't stand Teresa Brewer's voice.

A glance at the Hires Root Beer wall clock told me that it wasn't even nine yet.

After finishing our drinks, the girls decided to move on—to the Bowling Alley—to see what was going on.

The Bowling Alley?

In formals?

On Friday night, with men's bowling leagues in progress?

Not me. I had to draw a line and put my feet beyond it, heading in the opposite direction.

Outside, when I announced, "I'm going home," the girls seemed surprised. "I have to work tomorrow," I added, and quickly parted company with the colorful trio.

The moon sparkled like a new penny and every star in the galaxy seemed to glow like the sun. Nature had conspired to make me as conspicuous as an elephant on a tightrope. The distance from the café to home was only four blocks. Remembering the boys in the pickup and other guys who cruised the boulevard harassing girls, I walked against traffic so cars couldn't trail me. It was the opposite side of the street from my house, both sides familiar since childhood. I hadn't been a child since the night five months ago when my dad died. In a couple of weeks I would graduate and begin working full time at Penney's.

I passed the darkened library; Miss Walton had just locked the door. A few feet beyond lay a beaten path kids used as a shortcut from school to downtown and their homes in that area.

Across the street, The Dog Park had a similar path bisecting it from Ninth Street to Tenth Street. In the next block I passed the house that once served as the hospital, with the funeral home conveniently across the street. Just past the old hospital stood the Whale Lady's house—wearing a mantle of my childhood imagination.

I slipped off my shoes. My nylons had runs when I put them on but it didn't matter, being under a long dress. I wouldn't wear them again.

The air hung heavy with lilac. The aroma could have come from one yard or many. Lilac bushes were common as dandelions.

In no rush, I walked a block past our house and then crossed over and ambled back toward home. It was still early. I eased open the door to the porch, stepped inside, closed the door, and paused, waiting to see if Ma had heard me come in. The television was on, but she might have fallen asleep. Atop the television sat a sleek black panther with a low watt bulb in its backside that cast a glow toward the ceiling. It was supposedly bad for your eyes to watch television in a completely dark room.

I sank onto the daybed, careful so the old springs didn't squeak.

Time passed and I heard Ma get up and switch channels to the news. Ten o'clock, at last. Then she went to the kitchen, and on her way back to the parlor she paused by the open dining room door.

What if she came out? I'd say I just got home and sat down to rest.

But she went to the parlor, and I relaxed.

When the news ended, Ma turned off the television but did not go to bed like she always did after the news. She was waiting up for me. I would have to go in sooner or later. I chose later.

When I finally entered the dining room, Ma rose from the couch and came out to meet me. I don't recall our conversation, but I imagine it went something like this.

"Is the dance over?"

"Not quite. I left a little early."

"Were there other single girls?"

"A few."

"What do kids do after the prom?"

"I don't know. House parties, maybe. Stay up all night, go somewhere for breakfast."

A cartoon bubble over my head added: *Drinking. Driving around. Necking at the sandpit.*

Somehow that didn't sound like a romantic place after prom.

"So, did you have a good time?"

"It was okay."

Cartoon bubble answer: *I stayed about a half hour and then walked downtown and I've been hiding on the porch for more than an hour because this was the most embarrassing night of my life and I don't want to talk about it.*

To change the subject I might have told Ma about how the gym was decorated, and laughed about the boys in black face. Or described the gowns and who the couples were.

Finally, we went to bed.

I never told anyone about that night; not my sister; nor my friends, and certainly not my mother. This is the document of record.

Not until years later did I understand why I went to the prom and carried out the charade. On some level, I must have realized that this event struck Ma's fancy because she never attended a prom, and I was the first of her daughters to have the opportunity. Mother and daughter were at cross purposes.

She wanted the prom for me.

I went for her.

Christmas Collective

A String Of Lights

Nothing revives the past so completely as a smell that was once associated with it.

~ ~ Vladimir Nabokov

Some of my favorite memories of childhood Christmases stem from the scents of the season, beginning with imagined aromas emanating from the mail-order catalog that arrived in the fall. Amid the pages of enticing toys and games was a section showing a variety of nuts, in and out of the shell, colorful candies, and boxed chocolates. They looked so real that I could easily smell peppermint, lemon, butterscotch, raspberry, caramel, and the sickeningly sweet syrup surrounding chocolate covered cherries. The hard tubular candy with a picture in the center was a mystery. How did they get the picture in there?

Our tree came into the house a day or two before Christmas. Poppy waited to take advantage of lowered prices as the days dwindled. One year, a friend of his from the American Legion gave him the one they had used for their holiday party. Taller and fuller than the ones we usually had, it came partially decorated with silver icicles clinging to its branches. Set up in the parlor in a bucket of wet sand, the tree emitted a fresh pine scent.

After trimming the tree, we kids hung plastic wreaths and candles in the windows, set up a crèche of cardboard figures, and strung red and green construction paper chains from corner to corner of the dining room and parlor. One year, Ma decided that the tree should be on the enclosed front porch, so that it could be seen and admired by passersby. We kids were against it, but she got her way. The tree glittered on the porch instead of in the parlor. Sorry, Ma; I still say it was a dumb idea.

After supper on Christmas Eve, Poppy gathered us kids around the dining room table for a card game. Dealing the first hand, he warned, "I never lose a game of Rummy on Christmas Eve."

I don't recall if that proved true, but the boast gave him the upper edge and put us on our toes to watch every move. With everything else she had to do, Ma made a big bowl of popcorn, caramelized with spun corn syrup, or served a batch of homemade fudge or powdered sugar candy.

Sooner than the usual bedtime, the bubs who still believed in Santa were sent to bed. Then, packages were pulled from closets, the cedar chest, the garage, or the car trunk. A half hour or so later, after some pounding around outside, maybe on the roof, Ma called upstairs that Santa had come, and the little ones raced back down, hoping their wishes had come true. One year, Joe came over as Santa, but the twins recognized him.

The packages under the tree often had more than one name on them; things to be shared: Bingo and Checkers, jigsaw puzzles, a blackboard and chalk, Tinker Toys, Lincoln Logs, and a package of modeling clay divided into strips of blue, red, green and yellow (I still smell that clay). There might be a couple of Big Little books, or those books with a small picture in each corner and when you flipped the pages, fast, it was like a speeded up movie.

It went without saying that the electric football game and the wood burning set were for the boys, the miniature tea set and paper dolls for the girls.

Walking to Midnight Mass, the crisp cold air propelled us into the starry night, past darkened houses or those aglow with outdoor lights. Cars encumbered by tire chains clanked slowly past. The only other sound was that of our rubber boots squeaking on packed snow.

Inside the church, a nativity scene with child-size figures dominated a side altar. Father Berger, garbed in holiday robes and swinging a gold and jeweled incense burner, evoked the ancient rites of The Magi paying tribute to the Christ child. The blend of incense; candle wax; and cheap perfumes and shaving lotions that children had given their parents, was nearly intoxicating in the overheated church.

Ma rose at dawn on Christmas morning to begin preparing dinner, and we awakened to enticing scents wafting from the kitchen. We numbered about thirty for dinner. The dining room table was extended the length of the room to accommodate the adults. Highchairs and laps held babies; the overflow of children and teens surrounded the kitchen table. Another noisy holiday meal commenced, and ended.

These memories have become of a piece. Strung together like Christmas tree lights, they glow and bubble and flicker, brightening the recesses of my mind. Viewed through an elapsed time frame, they appear as idyllic as a Norman Rockwell painting. Although life is never that simple, perhaps that is how Christmas is meant to be remembered.

My string of lights is not without dark spots—two in particular. In 1952, Poppy's death two weeks before Christmas altered the parameters of our celebration. The family gathered, our already purchased gifts were exchanged, but there was little holiday cheer. Poppy's former boss, Dr. Robert Wahl, had stopped by to bring a package that Poppy had stored at the office. It was cowboy outfits for the twins, delivered by Santa.

In April of 1957, Ma died. By Christmas we were somewhat able to tuck away our sadness. We older members of the family pooled our money to buy the twins a special gift. Not all of my siblings were there when the red and white Firestone bicycle was rolled into the house, so they did not see the boys' surprised faces. As Ma had always been, I had my camera aimed.

In one black and white snapshot, Dennis is on the seat, while David kneels on the floor beside him. In the other, David has a turn on the seat, while Dennis sits on the back fender, watching his brother read the card that accompanied the gift.

Although the bicycle is long gone (as is David), the photos of the smiling boys keeps the memory alive, making it a gift that has lasted a lifetime. It's a pleasure to run across the snapshots. At a glance I am instantly returned to that one Christmas out of a collective of many.

Dennis on bike, and David, 1957

Simply Delicious

An apple a day keeps the doctor away.

~ ~ Unknown

Christmastime surrounds us with a potpourri of scents: fresh cut pine, gingerbread, eggnog, cinnamon, pumpkin pie, and a plump turkey stuffed with sage dressing roasting in the oven.

For me, the definitive scent of Christmas is apples. It drifts toward me from the 1940s, reminding me of a time when life was far different than it is today, when simple gifts were ever so special.

Just before Christmas each year, Uncle Bud stopped by our house with a wooden crate of apples, his gift for the family. Although we had little interest in our bachelor uncle, we awaited this visit. Finally one night after supper, a pair of headlights illuminated the back yard and cut a swath through the steamed over kitchen window.

Uncle Bud tapped on the glass pane in the back door and entered the kitchen, bearing his gift. Poppy thanked him and placed the box on the table. Uncle Bud's glasses fogged over and he removed them for a minute while he shucked his coat, hat, and gloves. He laid them neatly on a chair; there wasn't room on the row of hooks on the kitchen wall where we kids hung our coats, hit or miss.

The brothers retired to the parlor to visit and have a drink of holiday cheer, provided by Uncle Bud. They discussed the weather, which brought them to farming. Uncle Bud worked as a hired hand and Poppy still had an interest in the subject. Farming was pretty much at a standstill in December, with only cows to milk and livestock to feed, but the men weren't at a loss for conversation.

When Poppy began the rigmarole of building a cigarette, Uncle Bud offered his store-bought cigarettes laid out in neat rows in a metal case something like a woman's face powder compact. Poppy declined and continued rolling his own. Uncle Bud secured his cigarette in a brass holder and lit up. Poppy held his imperfect cigarette between nicotine-stained fingers. Circles of smoke floated upward.

Meanwhile, the gift box sat on the kitchen table atop the cracked and worn oil cloth.

The apples were as tempting as those in the Garden of Eden surely had been to Adam and Eve. These apples were not only tempting, they were forbidden fruit. Poppy always stashed the box under his and Ma's bed in the downstairs bedroom, and we'd been told that we could not help ourselves. Given free rein, we would have gone through the box like a swarm of grasshoppers in a cornfield.

It's not that we never had fruit. We had an apple tree in the backyard, which bore tasty produce after we cut around the worm holes and bruises caused by a fall to the ground and where birds and squirrels and ants and bees had feasted. But summer had long passed, and with it the fruits of the season. The Christmas apples were special; perfect, uniform in size, shiny and polished, each nestled in a Prussian blue tissue paper blanket.

Poppy doled out the apples as bedtime treats, cutting them in half with his pocket knife to stretch them further. A half apple was better than none, and we were not disappointed in our nightly portion. We broke through the rind, sank our teeth into the pulp and gnawed our way to the core and seeds. Each crisp and savory bite lived up to the name Delicious.

Shirley and I saved the wrappers, first ironing them and then using them to make Christmas decorations or paper doll dresses. We tucked a few tissues into drawers for a sweet sachet. Later, we lined Easter baskets or May baskets with them. Now and then, the used wrappers added a hint of cidery fragrance to the warm, dry, indoor air of winter and early spring.

It was apple harvest time in Virginia, where I lived when I received word that Uncle Bud had died. Miles and years removed from the place and time when I was a child, the aroma of his gift wafted over me.

The scent of apples remains a comforting year-round memory, evoked when today's hectic pace and focus on expensive products makes me yearn for the simplicity of an era long past.

Simply Delicious was my first published piece, in 1985. It has since been published many times.

In Keeping With Christmas Past

On Christmas around 8:00 P.M., my whole family was in my house, opening their presents. Every body was excited, Surprze and did a lot of expressions! (I like that!) I opened two books, a horse that you can paint, a toy horse with a doll. (The horse can carry me.) But my favortie one was the GLOBE! The globe is glow in the dark. It shows the stars and constellations. But you can still see the continents and countries. The map key is lage. I love my Christmas present.

~ ~ Grace Linnet Buzby, age nine, author and illustrator of *What If I had a Pet Gator? And other stories!*, Barrett Elementary School
2011-2012

The Salvation Army's holiday donation drive is a long-standing tradition. The unobtrusive manner of the workers and the merry tinkle of their hand bells is all it takes to make me reach into my pocket. In addition to the familiar red kettles, the Salvation Army erects angel trees in shopping malls. Each paper angel lists a child's given name, sex, age, identification number, clothing sizes, and a wish list. Shoppers choose an angel and place packages under the tree for that child.

My small hometown in Iowa has a similar program, called Sharing Christmas. The weekly newspaper lists participating families by number only, along with their wish list, mostly basic items that many of us take for granted. Family #7 would like a grocery box and boy's thermal underwear, sizes 10 and 12. Family #23 woman needs a pair of overshoes, size 8, husband needs a sweatshirt, extra large, and warm work gloves. Family #30 needs baby formula, and flannel pajamas for girl, size 4. One little girl wished for a hairbrush. Imagine a child not having a hairbrush. Some lists include the latest popular toy or game, but those requests read like an afterthought, as if it might be considered frivolous for a child from a needy family to wish for an expensive toy. Some requests opt for the food box.

The Sharing Christmas program and Angel Trees are reminders of my childhood. Like many families during the Depression and thereafter, we were monetarily poor. At Christmastime, we received a food box from the town's Community Chest.

By Christmas Eve afternoon our house was dressed for the holiday. The fragrant pine tree in the parlor, propped in a bucket of wet sand, held homemade ornaments and strung popcorn. Lead icicles sparkled in the soft glow of blue, red, and green bulbs hidden in the branches. A worn cardboard crèche sat on a table (one of the three Magi had long been missing); a lighted plastic wreath hung lopsided in the kitchen window, its electrical cord dangling to the nearest socket. Strung corner to corner of the dining room ceiling were red and green construction paper chains we kids had cut and pasted together. The heat from the room often loosened the chains and they had to be rehung time and again.

Ma bustled about the kitchen making stuffing from dry bread, onions, and sage, or rolling piecrusts. I caught the dough she trimmed from the crust after she pressed it into a tin. I patted the scraps into small pies, sprinkled them with brown sugar and cinnamon, and popped them in the oven.

"When will the box come?" one of us kids periodically asked.

"It'll come when it comes," was Ma's unsatisfying answer.

As the afternoon drew to a close, the sky became splashed with variegated colors bleeding together like a child's watercolor painting. Drying her hands on her apron, Ma walked to the window and called, "Santa spilled his buckets of paint."

We scurried from all directions, wondering aloud which of the many colors sprinkled across the horizon had been used for the toys Santa would bring. Had he finished painting before the buckets tipped over? Was this his way of showing us that he had finished his job, that all was ready for that flight from afar?

"When will Santa come?" a little brother asked.

"Not until you're asleep," Ma said.

"When will the grocery box come?"

"Before long." She went back to work and, sure enough, within minutes the delivery truck lumbered around the corner, its tire chains squeaking on packed snow.

The box was delivered by our neighbor, at whose grocery store some of the food was purchased. He and Ma visited for a moment, she thanked him, and they wished each other a Merry Christmas as he left.

We kids gathered around the table. From the box Ma pulled a turkey, a pound of butter (a glorious treat for oleomargarine users), a one pound can of coffee, a jar of pimento olives, a can of jellied cranberry sauce, a clump of celery whose leafy top smelled as fresh as spring, several warty sweet potatoes, and cans of mincemeat and pumpkin that would become pie before Ma's work day ended.

"That's everything," she said, closing the lid.

I knew that wasn't everything. In the bottom of the box were goodies for our stockings: ribboned candies, nuts in the shell, and fragrant oranges. Fresh fruit during Iowa's severe winters was expensive, so oranges were as welcome as St. Nick himself.

Today, reaching back to my Midwest roots, and in my parents' name, I donate to the Sharing Christmas program in the small community that once nurtured my family. I do it for the kids who might be waiting at the window, wondering when the delivery will come.

And I pluck an angel from the Salvation Army's tree. My latest angel was Maria. I'll never meet Maria, but I know her; she's the child I used to be. I'll wager that Maria, and the scores of children whose names appear on the trees, will someday, in one way or another, sponsor angels of their own, in keeping with Christmas past.

A Most Distinguished Effect

The perfect Christmas tree? All trees are perfect!
~ ~ Charles N. Barnard

There are as many ways to trim a Christmas tree as there are snowflakes in a blizzard. How you do it probably has something to do with family traditions and rituals from Christmases past.

Some people prefer an eclectic approach, glazing the greenery with colorful ornaments and trinkets collected over a lifetime. Each familiar piece is a stepping stone to an earlier era, evoking a string of memories tied together like the lights on the tree. At the top there is often a star or an angel.

Others like a color-coordinated tree, perhaps with only white lights and gold ribbons, or a theme tree laden with Santa Claus figures, snowmen, miniature toys, or collectible items from a classic movie such as *Star Wars* or *Lord of the Rings*. One year, in lieu of my traditional eclectic tree, I used an African theme, with carved animals to catch the eye of my granddaughter visiting from South Africa. Breaking with tradition, the tree had no tinsel for the inquisitive toddler to pluck off and possibly eat.

When it comes to tinsel, there are two kinds of people; those who cry, "No, never," and those who claim a tree isn't complete until the silvery threads are added, "One at a time, please."

I'm among the latter; my daughter stands with the former. Still, one year she gave me two unopened envelopes of vintage lead icicles, the kind used when I was a child. Dull silver in color, each strand has enough weight so that when hung on the tree, it stays put. Today's flimsy plastic particles create static electricity and float about in the slightest air current.

Humorist Russell Baker appreciated lead icicles. In a column he wrote years ago, he revealed that his wife and children think icicles are vulgar. He explained, "That's the whole point. Of course icicles are vulgar. Christmas trees are vulgar, too, and in bad taste. Putting a chopped pine in the parlor is almost as tasteless as putting a plastic one in the parlor, and the reason we do it is because Christmas is the only holiday we have that authorizes even the fanciest people to revel in vulgarity and bad taste."

Tinsel originated in Germany in about 1620. In the late 1800s, German glassblowers produced crystal ornaments that looked like actual icicles, with a built-in hook for hanging them. In darkened Victorian parlors, trees sparkled with these glass, tin, or sterling silver icicles. Along about 1920, lead tinsel was introduced. The product was banned from the market in 1960 to protect children from lead poisoning should they chew the strands. At that time, Russell Baker bought all the lead icicles he could find and hoarded them in his attic.

Alas; I didn't do that, but I have the two packages from my daughter. They originated in Germany, probably in the 1930s. On the brown paper envelopes are the words: *Brillant Eis-Lametta. Vornehmste a. effectvollste Zierde des Weihnachtsbaumes.*

Loosely translated that means: Brilliant ice-tinsel. Most distinguished, fullest effect for your Christmas tree.

Shimmering on my tree, they do indeed create a distinguished effect. Carefully removed and stored each year, they should last another century. And since Christmas is mostly about nostalgia and tradition, perhaps one day my grandchildren will drape my vintage icicles on their trees. They might explain to their children, "We'll do it for Granny. She always put gobs of tinsel on her Christmas tree."

Stepping Into Her Shoes

In Her Easter Bonnet

The fashionable female hat is nothing, after all, but a caprice. Let those who pay for it, fifty dollars, more or less, grumble about the cost. We, as spectators, shall be satisfied if it prove an ornament.

~ ~ Harper's Weekly, 1857

During the brutal winter of 1956-57, Ma wrote to my sister:

Boy it is sure cold here today. I never had such a cold house as we have had this winter. I believe before next winter I'll move into an apartment or somewhere where your heat is furnished. Dolores wanted to know why I didn't come down a couple days & stay. I'm going to as soon as the weather gets warmer but I hate to leave when it's so cold, with the fires [our oil burner] so hot & everything. I'm so afraid of fires.

Spring finally arrived; April showers cleansed the air and left it scented with fruit blossoms and lilac. People had begun preparing and planting their gardens. An Irish adage had it that if you hadn't planted potatoes by St. Patrick's Day, don't bother; it was too late. Poppy had always put in a large plot of seed potatoes (chunks of potato with eyes that would sprout), but after his death Ma did only her usual vegetables. Ordinarily, by this time, she would have planted carrots, green beans, cucumbers, lettuce, onions, peas, cabbage, beets, red and white radishes, fragrant dill for making pickles, and lots of tomato plants. There might be sweet corn, too, and then a line of hollyhocks at the alley end of the garden. The main portion of our summer meals came fresh from the garden, with some of the produce canned and stored for winter. In late summer, Poppy bought crates of peaches and pears for canning, and some of the apples from our tree went into sauce and apple butter.

But this spring Ma had been ordered by her doctor to do nothing strenuous. She could, of course, plant her window box outside the dining room window or weed the tiger lily beds along the boulevard. She and Iris would drive into the country and gather tender sprigs of asparagus from along the ditches, but there would be no vegetable garden. I hadn't the knowledge, nor the time. Odd that I should say that; Ma had time all those years, in the midst of raising a big family. All I'd learned as a child about gardening was pulling weeds and picking potato bugs off the plants.

To a woman who, since her marriage at eighteen, had seldom known an idle moment, nor had time to pursue a hobby, doing nothing was a skill Ma had not acquired. She read romance magazines, listened to radio soap operas, and watched television: Arthur Godfrey, *The Breakfast Club, Queen For A Day, Art Linkletter's House Party*, and game shows.

As she'd promised my sisters, Ma rode the bus to Sioux City and spent a few days with them. Back home, on the Wednesday before Easter, she walked downtown to pass time visiting with friends at the Palace Café. Glenn and Ruth Johnson now owned the place and she liked them both.

It was an easy walk; five blocks on flat terrain. On her way home, she stopped to see me at Penney's, where I worked in Ladies Ready-To-Wear. After climbing the stairs to the second floor, she was out of breath so she sat on a stool in front of the three-way mirror at the hat counter.

Standing behind her, I placed hats on her head. Small hats, large hats, wide-brimmed hats, fabric hats, straw hats, plain hats, and hats adorned with bows, streamers, lace, veils, plastic flowers and dyed plaster fruit. We laughed at some of the creations.

Female Catholics were required to cover their heads inside the church, so hats were not just fashion statements, they were a necessity. An Easter bonnet heralded the celebration of spring.

Donning a small hat, Ma looked in the mirror and turned left, right, forward again, checking the view from all angles.

"You should buy it," I suggested.

"Oh, no," she said, "my navy hat is fine. I'll wear my navy suit to Easter mass."

When she glanced at the price tag, I said, "I could buy it and get my discount."

She seemed to consider the offer, but then said, "No; I don't need a new hat."

A customer came up the stairs and Ma left.

The next evening, Joe's oldest girls came to the house to have supper with Grandma, the three boys, and me. Then I took the twins and the girls to Holy Thursday service at church. Ma didn't feel up to going and hoped that God would forgive her.

Sometime during the night or early morning, she died in her sleep. It was Good Friday.

That day in the store, trying on hats, remains my favorite memory of the two of us together.

Maybelle, circa 1955

Mother's Day

A mother is she who can take the place of all others but whose place no one else can take.

~ ~ Cardinal Gaspard Mermillod (1824-1892)

When Mother's Day arrived just weeks after Ma's death, the twins presented me with construction paper cards they'd made in school. David's was a white sheet folded in half. Printed on the front, among red roses, was: On Mother's Day. Inside, was a handmade coupon reading:

For Mother's Day: Appreciation Ticket
This ticket is good for a housecleaning job.
Signed: David
(I'm worth my weight in gold.)

Below that was a poem:

To Madonna:
It really is a pleasure
To greet you on "your" day
For you're a precious treasure
Worth more than words can say.

Dennis's card was on yellow paper, cut in half and folded like a commercial greeting card. A construction paper blue tulip adorned the front. Inside was this poem:

The Best of Sisters

Hundreds of stars in the pretty sky
Hundreds of shells on the shore together
Hundreds of birds that go singing by
Hundreds of lambs in the sunny weather
Hundreds of dewdrops to greet the dawn
Hundreds of bees in the purple clover
Hundreds of butterflies on the lawn
But you're the best sister the wide world over.

Love, Dennis

I have no recall of my reaction to their offerings. Today, when I come across the cards I think how difficult it must have been for the boys, making cards for their sister while the other kids were writing to their mothers.

I hope their teachers were sensitive and guided them quietly.

In 1966, I celebrated my first Mother's Day with my baby daughter. I've had many lovely Mother's Day celebrations since, but none have the nostalgic poignancy of that long ago Sunday in May.

The First Step

Memories,
Light the corners of my mind
Misty watercolor memories
Of the way we were ...

~ ~ Alan Bergman, Marilyn Bergman,
Marvin Hamlisch

My mother was fifty-four years and six weeks old when she died. My vision of her is so distant that it takes all of my senses and all of my recall power to convince myself that she was ever real. Lost in a shadowy aura I cannot penetrate, she lies just out of reach. As disconnected and unfocused scenes flip flop through my mind, it's like being at a movie in my youth when the film suddenly sputtered to a halt and the screen stayed dark until the film could be spliced and restarted. I always wondered: what did I miss, was there a scene cut? What is missing from the vignettes I splice together about my mother?

The last snapshot taken of her, on her March eleventh birthday, is grainy, slightly out of focus. She is seated at the dining room table propping up her birthday cake. With that image freezing her in time, I see a woman whose eyes are lively while her smile is hesitant. The smile helps me recall her laugh. She had a good sense of humor, but it seems to me she often tried to hold back from laughing, as if a belly-laugh was not dignified. When she failed to contain a laugh, it burst forth in a sputter. I can summon her voice, too, as I can Poppy's and those of my deceased siblings. Why do voices stay with us?

In the photo she looks pale, her skin smooth and unlined, her nose a bit too large for her face. She is not wearing her glasses. Her hair, parted in the middle and not quite to her shoulders, shows some gray. I'm reminded of how she used to invite us kids to comb her hair and pluck out the silver invaders. That's when there were only a few gray hairs; she later gave up fighting them. After a shampoo, she liked to have her hair set in pin curls, but was always disappointed in the outcome, complaining that her naturally wavy hair had a mind of its own. My hair does the same thing.

Although she looks tired in the picture, I don't see a woman who would die within weeks. But a stressful life had exacted a toll and reduced her life span. They used to say that a woman lost a tooth for every child, and years before Ma had been fitted with dentures. I remember her sometimes going to bed because of *sick headaches.* Migraine, maybe? She carried too many pounds on her slightly more than five-foot frame; her legs were disfigured by varicose veins, and now she had heart disease and hypertension.

Tangible evidence of her life is scattered among family households. Stitched together in my mind like one of her patchwork quilts, each piece affords warmth and comfort. I have her plain gold wedding band. Years ago I had the date engraved inside the ring. In her wedding photo she is wearing a cross around her neck. In a later picture of my grandmother, she's wearing a cross that looks similar. I wonder if the cross was my grandmother's, and perhaps Ma wore it as the traditional something borrowed.

Also visible in the picture is Ma's engagement ring, a diamond or sapphire; my older sisters were not sure. They recalled that on Sunday mornings Ma took the ring from the bureau drawer where she kept it and polished it with a cigarette paper before wearing it to Mass. Later, the ring disappeared. My oldest brother sometimes infuriated my oldest sister by teasing that she had taken the ring to school and traded it for a pork chop sandwich. Indignant, Billie asserted that Ma believed that a hired man stole the ring when the family was away from the house.

I have a rummage of Ma's dishes, bowls, Depression glass, and silver plate flatware. From her wake and funeral I have the Visitor's Register, a faded ribbon from a bouquet, Requiem Mass cards, sympathy cards, a list of food and cash given to the family, and a receipt for funeral expenses: $455.38. I have receipts from payments Ma made toward Poppy's funeral, and a receipt for a used black and white television set. I have her last eyeglasses with one broken stem. Having kept these items all these years, I can't discard them now. I'll leave that to someone with a far-removed connection to family relics.

My oldest sister had Ma's cedar chest, one of the few things that survived my sister's house fire. Her son has the chest now and perhaps it will go to his daughter. Shirley has a statue of the Virgin Mary (the one we used for a May shrine), my brother has a wooden bench made by Poppy, on which the youngest in the family sat at meals. A granddaughter has the two burner iron griddle on which Ma flipped countless pancakes.

When I returned home in 1956, Ma asked me to sleep with her. She worried that she might need help in the night and no one would hear her call. I slept beside her, but I could not help when death came a few months later.

I awoke that morning, Good Friday, and began dressing for work. Then I heard an unfamiliar sound coming from where

Ma lay in bed. It wasn't a snore, nor did it sound like she had said something. I would later describe it as a gurgle. I said, "Ma," a couple of times. There was no response. I knelt by the bed and shook her gently.

I knew then the meaning of the phrase *still as death*. "Oh, no," is what I said aloud.

I called Joe; he called the doctor and the priest before he and Iris came to the house. Joe said that Father Berger was away, but his substitute would come as soon as he finished saying Mass.

Dr. O'Leary's death certificate listed the cause of death as a coronary occlusion stemming from ten years of hypertensive heart disease. The date was April 19, 1957, the time: 8:00 a.m., the time of his examination rather than the approximate time I heard the gurgle. That left the priest within his rights to administer Extreme Unction; the belief being that the soul stays with the body for an hour after death.

We prepared for the priest's visit. Using the sick call set that had hung on the bedroom wall for years, we took from under the sliding panel on the back of the crucifix the items required for the sacrament. On a table covered with a white cloth we placed two lighted candles, a glass of water, six balls of cotton, some crumbled bread (or salt), and the crucifix. According to custom, I met the priest at the door and escorted him to the bedroom. Then I, Joe, Iris, and Danny, the oldest of my three brothers at home, knelt around the bed while Father Condon administered the final rite of passage.

As the funeral director and his helper carried my mother away, Iris, said, "It's so final." She dearly loved my mother.

I asked Danny to call my boss and tell him I wouldn't be in. Trusting in the lore that men are stronger than women; that men do not break down and cry like women do, I asked a boy to become a man and make the call. Hindsight tells me it must have been as difficult for him to speak the words as it would have been for me.

I had one task I could not shirk. I climbed the stairs and woke the twins. I don't know how they had slept through the commotion downstairs. In retrospect, it would have been better to have awakened them and brought them down, rather than have them walk into the scene unaware of what had happened.

Family members arrived from near and far, filling the house as if it were a holiday gathering, but without the cheer. Ma was not bustling about the kitchen in a printed cotton dress and wraparound apron. She was not head-over-heels in the oven basting a beef roast, her face blotchy from heat. She was not trying to visit with everyone at once, while bouncing a small grandchild on her hip. She was only an ethereal presence in our muddled states of mind.

A neighbor, Gladys Mauch, took the twins to her house to, "Take their minds off it." My older brothers left to select a casket and make funeral arrangements. We women put the house in order for the callers who would soon stream into the house bringing food and sympathy. We picked out a dress for Ma; gray with red trim. My sisters recalled that Poppy never wanted her to wear red or other bright colors. After his death, she chose dresses with a touch of gaiety.

On Easter Sunday, women from the Catholic Daughters took over our house, providing, cooking, and serving dinner. We were guests at our own table.

Of all the kindnesses paid our family, the dearest one came from our newspaper carrier, Georgie Fox, a playmate of the twins'. He knocked on the door on collection day, but when I held out the money he waved it away. "I'll get it this week," he said, handing me the receipt.

Taking comfort in the many shoulders on which to lean, we siblings cried together, shared our grief, prayed the rosary, overlooked Ma's faults and elevated her to near sainthood, as did others. In a letter to my aunt Goldie, one of the parish nuns wrote:

> I had one or two good talks with Mrs. Dries and I thought she was a lovely person. Surely with a life such as she lived, taking care of her children and even working to help them, she must have gotten quite a welcome when she met her Maker.

We wondered, and worried—what did I last say to Ma? Was it said lovingly? In anger? With indifference? Going back in time, what words had been uttered that should have been left unspoken? What had we neglected to say?

I love you.

If those words were ever spoken in our household, by parent or child, I have no memory of it. A greeting card verse spoke for us, or a sign-off at the bottom of a letter: Love —

I've been asked what it was like growing up in such a big family. I have nothing to compare it to; it might have been chaos, but it was normal for me. Although I have no recollection of ever being hugged by my parents, neither do I recall ever feeling that I was missing something. I never felt neglected or jealous that a sibling got more attention than I did. I don't recall ever having a birthday party, or a cake, or receiving gifts. That's not to say I didn't have those things; it's just not in my store of memories. Nor do I feel that I'm impaired by nostalgia. I simply have no quarrel with my childhood. My parents' love and concern are evident in memories of kind acts and sacrifices made for their children.

The first night after Ma's death, I awoke from a disturbing dream and went to the kitchen, where I found Dolores sitting in the dark, smoking a cigarette. I described the dream, in which something in the shape of a sphere, like a globe of the world, had been placed on my shoulders, pressing down on me. I don't know if we tried to interpret the dream; I was not then, nor am I now, big on what dreams mean. But did the sphere represent our family circle, now broken? Did the weight bearing down on me represent sorrow? Or the enormity of the task ahead of me? It had become clear that I would stay with the boys. I had taken my first steps onto the path leading to the next few years.

Dolores suggested that we go to bed. I said I was going to scrub the kitchen linoleum while no one was in the way. She told me the floor was fine, but I wasn't ready to go back to bed.

As I scoured the floor on my hands and knees, I recalled that I had heard my sister-in-law say that I had not yet cried, and that I would feel better if I did. Phoebe was wrong on both counts; I had cried, I was crying now, and I did not feel better. Tears could not wash away the disbelief and numbness of what had happened. The invisible umbilical cord that had stretched between Ma and her children had been severed, leaving us unanchored. I and my siblings, even those who were still children, were no longer the next generation; we were the elders.

My brothers and I would occupy the house along the boulevard, but it would not be ours alone. Other siblings would come and go and still call it *home*. The doors had never been locked, and wouldn't be now. I recall coming home after an evening out and finding the beds (even mine) filled with siblings and in-laws and nieces and nephews. This house would be the gathering place until two years later when I gave Uncle Bud notice that the twins and I were moving.

That house is nearly unrecognizable now for the renovations. A couple of my brothers have been inside and have described the changes, but my mind sees it the way it was when we lived there. Daryl told me, "Despite the changes, when I opened the door to the upstairs and put my hand on the railing and began walking up, everything about living there flooded back."

Who was this woman we called Ma? Was she merely a simple country girl, a wife and mother through and through, or had she dreamed of doing something else? Did she have latent artistic talent? Her black and white photographs tell me that she had a good eye for composing pictures, and for capturing a candid moment.

I've found traces of her personality in letters written to my older sisters. I'm grateful to them for having kept the letters, and envious that they had an adult relationship with her. Surely she wrote to Shirley and me during the year we spent away from home, but if she did I have none of those letters. The penned messages to my sisters allow access to Ma's intimate feelings, her grief and happiness, her humor, spirit, courage, and strength.

In a letter written after the birth of her eighth son, her first hospital delivery, she wrote that she and Poppy had had fun surprising folks, that no one knew she was expecting, not even her mother or sister (nor my sister, to whom she was writing). Then she admitted:

> I sure wish he was a girl. I was so disappointed I could have cried. We both wanted a girl, one with black hair like Toots, but he is just the opposite, almost has red hair. How's that for a scandal? But he is so good so there isn't anything to kick about. The kids all like him just as well as if he was the first one we ever had.

Given the Catholic church's dogma on birth control, common sense tells me that none of her pregnancies were planned. But in that letter her voice tells me that even after struggling to care for so many children, there was room and joy in her heart for another.

Eight months later, after the sudden death of this baby from pneumonia, she wrote to my sister:

> I don't think I ever put in such a lonesome week. I am just beginning to get my bearings. Everyone says it's better to put everything of baby's away, but I think I would feel better if I could see some of his things lying around. Oh well, I guess I'll get over it sometime. I hope.

Did guilt enter into her grieving? She had, after all, been disappointed that the baby was a boy. Did she believe God was punishing her?

I clearly remember the day he died. I was walking home from school when my not yet four-year-old brother came running up the street to meet me. Danny told me that Donny had died. Not believing him, I rushed into the house, where I found Ma lying on the sofa, crying. She asked me to go tell our neighbor, Mrs. Enright, that the baby had died, but I began crying and said I didn't want to. She didn't insist.

The small white casket sat in the parlor. Donnie was dressed in a white knit romper. A nun told me that he was now an angel in Heaven. I wanted to tell her that I didn't want an angel in Heaven, I wanted my brother, but children did not contradict nuns. I later sneaked into the room when no one was there, lifted the veil, and kissed his cold cheek. My siblings have told me they did this, too.

For a while, I believed his death was my fault. The weather was cold and I'd taken him out on the enclosed porch, without a coat or cap, and stood talking to a friend. As an adult, I realized I was not responsible.

Years after Ma's death, I found a poem she had clipped from a magazine and tucked into Donnie's baby book. Called *A Letter To God*, it's a mother's lament about the death of her baby son. It expresses feelings that Ma must have identified with but could not put into words.

After Poppy's sudden death in 1952, Ma wrote to my sister:

> It don't seem possible it will soon be a month since your dad is gone. It still seems like a dream. I miss him most from five o'clock on.

My parents' marriage was far from calm, but appearing here is a woman who loved her husband and who missed him coming home from work at day's end.

Two letters are particularly meaningful to me. After Christmas, 1956, Ma wrote to my sister:

> Seems like there was so much excitement at Xmas I didn't hardly talk to anyone or thank them for what they brought. I guess I'm getting old or something to not take a little excitement. My arms and legs hurt so Xmas night that Madonna rang the doctor and he said put ice packs on them. That was a job but it helped, along with aspirin. Doc said it was Christmas exhaustion. Ever hear of it?

The other letter was to Larry, in the Air Force in Japan, received by him after Ma died. She wrote:

> I don't know what I would do without Madonna. She does all the housework plus working at Penney's.

Those excerpts assure me that, in a small way, I did something to ease Ma's last six months. I have little recall of that period. What did we talk about? Did she express concerns about her health? Did it occur to her that I might end up raising my brothers? Did it occur to me?

This would have been the time for me to ask questions, to listen to her reminisce about the early days. This would have been the time to ask what I was like as a little girl, but at twenty-one, who is interested in reflecting on the past? That often comes later, as it did for me when my daughter wanted stories about when I was a little girl; when I no longer had parents to supply answers.

In this quote, from her last letter to my sister, I hear a woman who has optimistically accepted the hand dealt her:

> You have been asking what the doctor says about me, he never says anything, only that I can't go to work. Sometimes my blood pressure is up and sometimes down. I have been having a bad cough, that doesn't seem to do my heart much good, but the cough is better now. I shouldn't complain, I don't have anything painful.

Aunt Kate Guertin once wrote to me:

> Your mother was always smiling, took everything in her stride. She was a tough disciplinarian, but said she hardly ever had to spank her kids, just now and then she had to give someone a whack. I remember one night Don and I and your mom and dad went to a dance. We came home late and Sybella and Dolores were walking the floor with a crying baby. I don't know now which baby it was. They'd tried giving the baby a bottle of sugar water but that hadn't helped. Your mother, whose breasts were

heavy and hurting, sat down, laughed and said, "Seems like I'm always nursing one baby or another."

Only the oldest grandchildren remember my mother; some with only vague recall. The eldest grandchild, Kaye, fourteen when my mother died, says, "I adored Grandma. She was always sweet to me and was a true grandma in every sense of the word."

Kaye's brother Steve says, "I remember Grandma's flowered aprons. She seemed to always want to pick me up and hold me. She had a big lap and my mother would tell me to give her a rest, but she would not put me down. The other sharp image I have is from the day she died. I was at the tin shop when my mother took the call. We went to the back of the shop and she told Dad that his mother had died. I will always remember how his shoulders heaved and he shrunk, staring at his workbench. It was my first inclination that he was capable of crying. Being so young, I still believed that dads are superhuman."

Jean says, "I remember a polka dot dress and sitting on someone's lap and my eyes had a hard time focusing. Years later, when I saw a picture of her wearing a polka dot dress I thought maybe I was sitting on her lap and trying to focus on polka dots!"

Paula says, "I remember going to Grandma's house for Sunday dinner and running around in the kitchen."

Sheila says, "I don't remember much about that evening [Holy Thursday] except that I wanted to spend the night at Grandma's but Mom wouldn't let me because there was too much to do for Easter. I guess her decision was divine intervention."

Randi never knew her grandmother, but says, "This might sound spooky or freaky, but there are times when I feel her around me even though we never met."

I sometimes feel her presence, too. I'm reminded of her when I see my daughter sewing aprons, making quilts, and gardening. Now my young granddaughter is learning to sew and quilt. When I read on Facebook that my niece and her daughter in Utah are canning produce from their gardens, I see Ma standing over a hot stove, Kerr jars rattling in boiling water, tomatoes steaming as they cook. We enjoyed those tomatoes in the winter, used to make her special hamburger and rice.

I see Ma's likeness in several generations: My brother David had her gray-green eyes, as does his daughter, Rosie, and her daughter, Maya Isabelle. Ma's middle name was Isabella. Drop a few letters from Maya Isabelle and we have Maybelle.

Great-granddaughter Chris bears an uncanny physical resemblance to Maybelle. For a college paper in the 1980s, Chris wrote:

Ironically, the person who I feel has contributed the most to who I am is dead; I have never met her. I feel strongly that Maybelle lives on in a part of me. Although I have never seen her, physically, she helped make me what I am today, and my heart aches to hold this great-grandmother I never met, but love dearly. A great deal of the time she is my inspiration.

Now a wife, mother, grandmother, and a Nurse Practitioner, Chris adds:

I recall thinking that I looked like her and that when I got married I wanted to be surrounded by a big family, with lots of kids and grandkids, which I guess I equated with lots of love! I saw her as a caregiver and knew that I held that caregiver gene within me.

I admire among my mother's descendants a long line of independent, confident, intelligent, accomplished, nurturing women. They shoulder both social and personal challenges and deal with adversity, grief, and joy with the same spirit, determination, courage, and love of family as did Maybelle. She would be pleased to know them.

Over the years, rarely has a day passed that I haven't thought of my mother, and missed her. Her death catapulted me headlong into life and left me stumbling for a few years. Did I adequately fill her shoes? Only she could answer that.

Step by step, I found my way. Reflecting on what Poppy advised long ago about the jigsaw puzzle: Keep at it, piece by piece, I'm comfortable with how the pieces came together.

Last photo of Maybelle, March 11, 1957

{ RELATIVELY SPEAKING }

Finding My Grandmothers

*And so our mothers and grandmothers have,
more often than not anonymously, handed on
the creative spark, the seed of the flower they
themselves never hoped to see—or like a sealed
letter they could not plainly read.*

~ ~ *Alice Walker*

I knew only one grandparent, my mother's mother, Agnes O'Brien Guertin. Until I was forty, and began researching family history, all I knew about my paternal grandmother was her name, Anna Barbara Lenz Dries, and that she was the second wife for my grandfather, Joseph Matt Dries. His first wife and a young child had died. Of my great-grandmothers, and further back, I knew nothing, not even their names.

Through newspaper articles, obituaries, census records, and hiring a man in Germany to research my paternal ancestors, I learned the names of greats, great-greats, and so on, as far back as the 1600s. The names, first and middle, are repetitive, with various spellings and combinations of Anna, Margaret, Magdalena, Maria, Mary, Barbara, Catherine, Katherine, Katherina, and a few lone names: Theresa, Frances, Eva, Suzanne, Luzia, Pauline, and Elizabeth.

These women were Catholic. One family many generations back converted from Judaism to Catholicism. Most of the women raised large families and suffered the loss of one or more children.

In photos, Grandmother Dries has a severe look, with her hair pulled back. Her clothing is drab, but her bearing is regal. If I imagine her smiling, I see a woman who was downright pretty. My sister Sybella remembered Grandmother wearing long black dresses and black aprons. On family visits to the farm, Sybella and Dolores broke into giggles as they ran up the stairs onto the porch because Grandmother always made everyone who ate at her table kneel down afterwards to say the rosary. The two little girls knew they would have a problem being reverent.

My paternal great-grandmother, Anna Katherine Raetz Dries, appears in photographs to be as tiny as a child. In one photo, seated, her feet do not touch the floor. She looks nearly bald, but I imagine her gray hair was thin and pulled tight to the scalp. German immigrants to Wisconsin and then Iowa, Anna and her husband, Joseph Sebastian, raised twelve children. The couple celebrated their 60th wedding anniversary in 1915. On that occasion, when they renewed their vows at Mass, this was part of the newspaper account:

Anna Katherine Raetz gave her hand in marriage to Joseph Dries and from that day they have been together man and wife, true to the most sacred vows, living in the love and companionship these many years. What a glorious thought of its reality, the trials and tribulations ever overcome by both. They were together in one another's joys and sorrows and with each succeeding year their love and affection for one another grew.

Joseph died a year later, and Anna Katherine lived another six years.

Unable to trace my maternal female ancestors as far back as the paternal, I have fewer names. For the Irish: Agnes, Bridget, Mary, and Jane. For the French-Canadian and English: Mathilda, Sara, and Mary.

Rosary beads and a crucifix were my great-grandmother Bridget McLaughlin O'Brien's constant companions. Prayer guided her through the deaths of two children; one was struck by lightning. Seventeen years later, Bridget's husband was killed by lightning. When she was dying of cancer in 1913, she asked her daughter to bury her with a crucifix and a white lily in her hands.

My great-grandmother, Mathilda Jane Patterson Guertin, lived seven months past the age of ninety-three. Her husband and four of their fifteen children preceded her in death. She died only three months before her oldest son, my grandfather, Edgar, with whom she shared a birthdate.

Until having a stroke in 1939, which left her helpless, Grandma Jane, as she was called, had been healthy all her life and was known for her brilliant memory. She had done her own housework, read without glasses, and was proficient at fancy needlework. She saw many movies, but alleged that air-conditioned theaters caused her only illness in fifty years, some kind of flu.

Known by everyone in Lake Park, Iowa, the headline on Mathilda's obituary read: Grandma Guertin Dies Friday Evening. The story stated: *Her passing was quiet and without struggle as her slumber merged with eternal sleep.*

My favorite photo of Mathilda shows her sitting in a rocking chair in a grove. She's wearing a long dress, and her white hair is knotted on top of her head. The image lets me imagine sitting down in the grass and chatting with her. Oh, the tales she might have told. My oldest sister once described her as sweet and kindly and she loved having company. That's how she appears to me in photos.

It's never too late to become acquainted with grandparents you never met. Talk to those who knew them, collect their stories, and study their pictures. Their clothes, hairstyles, and body language will present clues to their personalities. Search for old obituaries. Today's obituaries tend to be only basic information, while vintage obits written in flowery prose are a font of personal data that brings life to the deceased person.

Celtic Runes

Let his memory live tho' his body be dead,
And may his name flourish whilst this can be
read.

~ ~ Irish epitaph

On a tree-lined knoll along a country road near the village
of Deerfield, Wisconsin, a cemetery marks the site where St.
Anne's Catholic Church had stood. Founded in 1855 to serve
Irish immigrants, the parish lasted only 20 years. By then most
of the settlers had migrated as a group to Iowa, lured by the
Homestead Act's free 160 acres of rich farm land.

Abandoned, the church deteriorated. It was razed in 1881.
With no caretaker for the cemetery, the ornate monuments
that stood as proud sentries over family plots became scarred
through time's vandalism. Assaulted for decades by rain, hail,
sleet, ice, wind, and fallen tree limbs, the moldering tombstones
crumbled, partially collapsed into hallowed ground. Strewn
across the field lay angels' wings, lost lambs, and broken
crosses, seasonally concealed by wild flowers and prairie grass
or buried under mounds of leaves or banks of crusted snow. The
inscriptions on the intact stones became embedded with soil
and moss, making them mostly illegible.

A century later, an article and photo in the *State Journal* verified that only a handful of markers remained. My brother, Vince, found one for a family ancestor.

John,
Son of
Patrick & Mary
McLaughlin
Died
January 14 1869
Aged 19 yrs 9 mo

Patrick and Mary McLaughlin were my great-great-grandparents. The words across the bottom of the marker had been scoured off, leaving what looked like ancient runic characters. Perhaps it was that old Irish favorite: Green be the turf above thee, friend of my better days, none knew thee but to love thee, nor named thee but in praise.

Or did the chiseled inscription reveal the cause of the young man's death? Did it name his birthplace, County Armagh, where the family lived before fleeing *An Gorta Mor* (The Great Hunger) in 1850? We'll never know.

In May of 1995, my niece, Jean Reiners Johnson, visited the cemetery and found John's headstone leaning against a tree, wild flowers and over grown grass surrounding it. A corner, with part of a cross visible, lay on the ground. Given that the entire place lay in shambles, with no indication that the grounds were being maintained, Jean took the corner of the tombstone as a keepsake. When she moved out of the country she gave the shard of granite to me.

One day while rummaging in a closet, I came across the relic. "How about putting this in the garden," I suggested to my husband, not really expecting it to fall into his landscape plan.

He liked the idea and found a place for the stone. Settled among plants, the artifact makes an interesting conversation piece as one approaches our door. More importantly, the simple stone grounds me in my Gaelic roots. Today, this shard might be all that's left of the many Celtic markers that once graced St. Anne's Cemetery in the village of Deerfield.

John McLaughlin stone

McLaughlin stone in garden

Hallowed Ground Restored

Go gcasaimid ar a chéile aríst
(Until we meet again)

~ ~ Gaelic epitaph

On my niece Jean's visit to the cemetery she also found the top half of Jane Reed O'Brien's headstone and others arranged in a mini-Stonehenge formation. Jane was my great-great-grandmother. She married Henry O'Brien in Ireland, and they emigrated to this country in 1850, along with twenty-year-old Susan and ten-year-old Henry, Jr.

The McLaughins emigrated at this time, too, and both families settled in the Boston area. Later, they moved to Deerfield, Wisconsin. Henry O'Brien, Jr. married Bridget McLaughlin, a sister to John, whose stone is featured in the previous story.

Jane Reed O'Brien (1790-1860)
Henry O'Brien, Sr. (1790-1868)

Just before submitting this book to the publisher I learned that St. Anne's Catholic Cemetery has been restored. The renewal was spearheaded by Eagle Scout Nick Collar of Deerfield's Troop 88.

Although Nick has no family connection to the cemetery, one day in 2010, driving past the ruins, he decided something should be done. He devised a plan and enlisted help from individuals, businesses, and his church. Within months, the team completed the work.

Dealing with 129 years of neglect, they cleared the wooded area that had encroached on the grounds—removed trees, limbs, and brush, sprayed weeds, and seeded the area with new grass.

That was only aesthetics. Nick wanted to restore or replace headstones and locate where they belonged. It was believed that there are 25 to 30 graves, but with the markers broken and scattered, no one knew where they belonged. The Madison Catholic Diocese found a hand drawn map from 1970 showing where some of the sites are located. It also showed the footprints of where the church stood.

With that in hand, Nick sought help from civil engineer Jeff Quamme and his company, Vierbicher & Associates. They surveyed the area and covered it with ground penetrating radar. This showed the location of the graves. Nick says that while the map is not official and he can't guarantee accuracy, when they began carefully digging in those areas they hit tombstone foundations. After piecing together broken headstones, like a giant jigsaw puzzle, Pechmann Memorials in Madison assisted in repairing, refinishing, or replacing the markers. Those with names were put in place according to the map. John McLaughlin's partially restored stone stands proudly upright again.

Eric Gestland, artist and assistant Eagle Scout master, created a sign, designed by Nick. Lastly, the cemetery needed to be assigned to a church, for maintenance. The church Nick attends in Cambridge, St. Pius X Catholic Church, accepted responsibility.

In addition to the already mentioned individuals and businesses that donated time, services, and funds, credit goes to Deerfield Farmer's Co-op; Deerfield Lions Club; and Unilock Corporation of Elkhorn.

Nick Collar's thoughtfulness and diligence is a gift to the community as well as to the families whose ancestors lie beneath the Wisconsin soil that many of them tilled more than a century ago.

Nick told me, modestly, "Sometimes when I drive past, I'm kind of impressed."

I'm highly impressed, and told him so.

Lightning Strikes Twice

Struck by lightning.

Those were frightening words to me, growing up in Iowa in the 1940s. Fierce thunder and lightning storms, or twisters that uprooted enormous trees, sent us scrambling to the storm cellar. It was there that Ma sometimes mentioned that her grandfather had been killed by lightning. "And little Essie, too," she added, speaking the words "little Essie," with a kind of reverence.

My mother's grandfather was too far back in time for me to imagine him as a real person, but "little Essie" intrigued me. From what I gathered, she was taking lunch to her father in the field when they were both killed by lightning. I envisioned this little girl, perhaps my age, skipping through the field, and then being struck down. Who died first, daughter or father?

It wasn't until years later, while doing genealogy, that I learned the full story. I also learned a valuable lesson—oral recitations are not always correct. Using my great-grandfather's name, his death date, and the information that he had been killed by lightning near Britt, Iowa, I wrote to the *Britt-News Tribune*. Britt is a small community, and surely such an event would have been worthy of an account in the paper. Indeed it was.

I received a copy of the obituary, written in the flowery prose common in those days. When I finished reading about my great-grandfather's life and death, my eyes were filled with tears. I felt as if I had met him and then lost him, within minutes.

August 5, 1909: Struck by lightning and instantly killed at the farm of his son, Linford, 7 miles northwest of Britt, August 5th at 5:45 p.m., Henry O'Brien, at the age of 70 years, 1 month, 11 days. Mr. O'Brien and his son had been in the harvest field all day, but were compelled to leave hurriedly at 5:30 p.m. on account of an approaching storm. The old gentleman was driving when, suddenly, without a moment's warning, he was hurled from this earth to eternity by a tremendous bolt of lightning which struck him in the back of the head, throwing him from the wagon among three prostrate horses which were also stunned.

The lengthy story related that the son, shocked, too, jumped from the wagon to aid his father, "but he was even then beyond recall." Oddly, there was no mention of the child Essie. It wasn't until I received another obituary for Henry O'Brien that the pieces fit. This brief account stated: Twelve years ago a daughter was killed by lightning near Garner.

She hadn't died at the same time as her father. A bit more research netted me Essie's obituary. It turned out her death had been seventeen years earlier, not twelve as stated in her father's obituary.

Garner, Hancock County Iowa, 28 July 1892: Hester Kate O'Brien, daughter of Henry O'Brien who lives on the old Cusick place, was killed by lightning yesterday afternoon about four o'clock. She was a bright little girl, about twelve-years-old, and was a general favorite with all who knew her.

Perhaps it's true that lightning doesn't strike twice in the same place, but it struck twice in the same family, a rare coincidence, it seems to me.

Henry and Bridget McLaughlin O'Brien

Gone But Not Forgotten

Do not regret growing older. It is a privilege denied to many.

~ ~ Unknown

A decade after writing *Lightning Strikes Twice*, and publishing it in *Family Tree* magazine (December 2002), an event occurred that added additional poignancy.

First, let's briefly recap the original details.

Essie O'Brien was buried near Garner, Iowa, where the family lived at the time. Her gravesite quite likely is lost to time.

Henry O'Brien was buried in St. Patrick's Cemetery near Britt, Iowa, where he had farmed. His wife, Bridget McLaughlin O'Brien, died in 1913 and was buried beside him. A year later, Alice Hahn joined her parents there. A small metal plate stuck into the ground marked each of the three graves. On Henry's and Bridget's markers, their birth years were incorrect.

More than a century later, the O'Brien's great-great-granddaughter, Dawn Foley Huisenga, visited the cemetery in Britt and found the markers cast aside. She returned them to their proper place, but she couldn't forget about them.

At a family reunion, Dawn began a collection to purchase a permanent headstone bearing all three names, the O'Brien's and their daughter's. For the design, she requested a rosary wrapped around a crucifix, and a lily. The idea came from Bridget O'Brien's obituary in the *Mason City Times.*

Mrs. O'Brien suffered intensely for five months with cancer. Her faithful companion at all times was her rosary and her crucifix. She made a request of one of her daughters to have a white lily and a crucifix in her hand when she was buried.

On Memorial Day weekend, 2011, three generations of the Foley clan (my cousins) traveled to Britt to dedicate the headstone. The sky loomed overcast and it rained in the morning—a reminder of the stormy afternoon when, seven miles away, a farmer in the harvest field *"was hurled from this earth to eternity."* But as the group gathered, sunshine broke through.

Dawn read Henry's and Bridget's obituaries, and Mary Foley Palmer recited a prayer and spoke about how God works through families.

"The commandments remind us to honor our mother and father, and we are honoring our great-great-grandparents with our ceremony today."

The relatives then held hands and recited The Lord's Prayer.

The patriarch, Roger Foley, said, "It's great that our kids would think about something like this. The history was new to me and it was great to find out about all of this. It was a touching story about the rosary, crucifix and lily, and I was happy to see it on the headstone."

Roger's daughter, Cynthia Ramirez, added, "It was a wonderful day. I wondered what Bridget and Henry would think—a hundred years later—their great, great-great, and great-great-great grandchildren dedicating a headstone for them. It was a proud feeling. I believe they were looking down and smiling on us."

Great-great-granddaughter Karen Teeselink commented, "I was telling my daughter their story and my granddaughter was fascinated that these were also her relatives. She wants to do her own family tree, and I'll be happy to help her on her journey."

An old adage claims that people are less afraid of dying than they are of being forgotten. Thanks to devoted genealogists in every generation, many of us have not—and will not—be forgotten.

Old O'Brien markers

New O'Brien marker

Gramma Might Have Told Me

Grandmas don't just say,"That's nice." They reel back and roll their eyes and throw up their hands and smile. You get your money's worth out of grandmas.

~ ~ Unknown

My maternal grandmother, Agnes O'Brien Guertin, lived in a one-room shanty that sat along a graveled road at the north edge of Sibley. The ceiling hung so low that medium sized adults needed to stoop when inside. As a child in the 1940s, the cottage suited me; I felt like a doll in a dollhouse.

When I visited Gramma on summer afternoons, I often found her on the front screened porch, sewing aprons or night gowns from feed sacks. She hummed as her head bobbed up and down over the sewing machine; up when the material glided along smoothly, down to inspect a seam or tear a thread with her teeth. I sat on the floor watching the treadle dance under her foot, staring boldly at the bunions protruding from holes cut in her felt slippers.

The pedaling stopped, and Gramma muttered, "Darn bobbin's empty again."

She leaned back and tugged combs and hairpins from her hair. At seventy her hair was still mostly dark. She pulled back the locks, damp with perspiration, and refastened a knot at the back of her head. Rising from her chair, she said, "Fetch a pail of fresh water and I'll make nectar."

Off I jogged to the pump in the neighbor's yard. I lugged back the enamelware pail using both hands, sloshing water on my bare feet and on the worn linoleum.

Gramma filled a clear glass pitcher with water and added a dollop of cherry syrup. As I watched the water swirl red and white like a barber's pole Gramma tossed in sugar; stirred, tasted, added sugar, stirred and tasted again. When satisfied, she used a long-handled dipper to fill two glasses.

I took both drinks while she reached into the cupboard and brought out a handful of sugar cookies, lightly browned around the edges. We went to the porch, where, seated in rocking chairs, we nibbled and sipped.

Outside, honey bees buzzed among the morning glories and four o'clocks, seeking sweet nectar of their own.

Gramma pointed across the road. "Look at that big kid galloping around on a mop, pretending he's Gene Autry."

I knew the boy from school. He was my age and I saw nothing wrong with playing Gene Autry. He was my favorite movie cowboy. But I laughed along with Gramma because she thought he was funny.

A pickup truck rattled by, stirring up dust that filtered through the screen on a gust of the ever present Iowa wind. A fat housefly circled our heads, droning like an Army bomber. Gramma picked up the mesh swatter, but laid it down when the fly collided with the sticky paper strip dangling above our heads.

The boy across the street called, "Whoa, Champion," and dismounted his mop horse and went inside.

"I guess Gene's going into the saloon for a drink with the other buckaroos," Gramma said.

I remember only that one conversation with her. I often wonder what else we discussed when I visited her.

I imagine a discussion something like this:

"Tell me about the olden days," I probably said.

"How olden?"

"When you were a little girl."

She might have begun with her grandparents, the McLaughlins, who fled Ireland during the potato famine and eked out a living in the Boston area before moving to a farm in Wisconsin. Then came the wagon journey when Gramma's grandparents and her parents moved to Iowa, in 1879, when Gramma was six. She might have talked about dust storms, grass fires, and tornadoes that swept across the nearly treeless prairie.

"Lightning, that's the worst. Papa and my sister Essie were killed by lightning."

"Really? At the same time?"

"No; that's what makes it remarkable. Essie in eighteen ninety-two; she was only twelve, and Papa in nineteen aught nine, in the harvest field. My brother Linford was there. He was stunned by the jolt, but he brought Papa home in the wagon. 'Hurled from this earth to eternity,' is what the paper said about Papa."

"Who was he to me?"

"He'd be your great-grandfather, Henry O'Brien."

She might have gone inside for her photo album and showed me his picture, with his wife. "Bridget was Mama's name. She died four years later, a painful death from cancer. But she never complained. She was buried with her rosary and crucifix and a white lily."

"Who's that baby picture?"

"That's Hester. We called her Essie."

"The one who got killed? Were you a little girl when she died?"

"I was eighteen. A year later, I married Ed."

I have no memory of my grandfather. He died when I was four.

"What was my mother like when she was little?"

"Oh, Maybelle was shy, quiet, like you. She had lots of friends and she loved babies. My goodness, she'd walk miles to see a new baby. Now she has a houseful of her own."

Gramma might have showed me pictures of her brothers, whose band played at barn dances where she and her sisters and friends gathered. And her cousins, four Jones sisters, members of a popular all-girl band in the 1930s, who later gave up show business to enter the convent with their widowed mother. "All five at the same time," Gramma would have explained. "Imagine that."

That might have led to a story about a McLaughlin cousin, Clem, who disappeared in the 1920s. "Married with three daughters. Folks say he ran off with a young girl who disappeared the same day. Clem borrowed his brother's car and called him the next day to say the car was at the Fargo depot. They must've got on the train and went somewhere. Nobody heard from them again."

After a while, I suppose I grew bored, as children do when old folks reminisce about people whose names mean nothing.

Forgotten until years later, when my parents were deceased and I began searching for my ancestors. Forgotten until I began to study old photographs and read old obituaries, wishing I could recall what I'd heard about these people; details that would bring life to the names on my genealogy charts.

In questioning relatives, I learned things that neither Gramma nor anyone else would have told me when I was a child. My older sister revealed that Aunt Arlowene was not our aunt, but our first cousin. Gramma and Grandpa raised her after their daughter, Gladius, gave birth out of wedlock. If my grandparents knew who the father was, no one else in the family ever learned his identity, not to this day.

Grandpa Guertin's family supposedly figured in a horse thief tale in Canada. But no one knew, or was willing to relate, details of the story. That family skeleton grows dusty in the closet.

I asked Uncle Jack Guertin if it was true he'd been a bootlegger. Grinning, he said, "I might've done some of that during the Depression. A fella had to make a living one way or another."

I found information about the Jones sisters of the all-girl band, and contacted them. They provided me with information about their career, as well as pictures and newspaper clippings. I learned from them that their uncle Clem had never been found. Not until 2008 did we learn the full story, and the sisters were deceased by then. (Their story is told in my book, *Swinging Sisters*.)

To Aunt Goldie Foley I said, "I remember hearing about someone who worked as a housekeeper for Mark Twain."

She laughed. "In our family? That's a new one on me."

If Aunt Goldie didn't know, no one would.

"Who was the girl who died just before her wedding and was buried in her bridal gown?"

Aunt Goldie thought for a moment. "Oh, yes, that was on your dad's side. She was to marry your dad's younger brother. Her name was Emma. Or was it Elsie? That doesn't sound right either. Hmm, what was her name?"

Aunt Goldie couldn't remember.

But Gramma might have told me on one of those quiet afternoons when we drank nectar and nibbled cookies and visited on her screened porch.

This story was published in Silver Boomer Books' anthology: *From The Porch Swing: memories of our grandparents.*

Guertin family circa 1910: back row left to right, Jack, Goldie, Leon, Gladius, front, Edgar, Donald, Agnes, Maybelle

Gramma And Granny

A house needs a grandmother in it.

~ ~ Louisa May Alcott

Gramma left the house and headed south, her hand in her apron pocket, jingling coins as she walked. She ended up at our house, about a mile in distance. After eating dinner with us, my father drove her back to my aunt Goldie's house, where Gramma lived. She stayed there until the next morning, when she walked back to our house again.

That might sound like a pleasant daily outing, but it worried Ma and Aunt Goldie. Their mother had become senile; childish they called it then.

"I can't take care of Mama any longer," Aunt Goldie told my mother one day in 1953. "She's lost her mind and she wanders off all the time. I'm afraid she'll get hurt."

Aunt Goldie and her husband both had health problems. My mother, recently widowed and with children to raise by herself, and health problems of her own, was in no position to tend her mother's needs, either. Nor could her two married sons who lived in town (I don't know their reasons). Another son and daughter lived away from the area.

My mother and her siblings talked about what to do, meanwhile Gramma stayed with Aunt Goldie. My mother wrote to my sister, Billie:

Mama has us all about run ragged. She's been chasing around from one place to another. She don't know one from the other. She was here over night lately and when she got up she didn't know where she was. When she gets into bed with me she asks where Frank will sleep. She doesn't remember that he died. We took her to Sanborn Friday to visit Aunt Annie [Gramma's sister]. Aunt Annie says she could stay there all the time, but Mama isn't satisfied after a few days. I and some of the others suggest to put her in Old Folks Home but Goldie has a fit. So we don't know what to do. She drives you nuts to have her around, she asks the same things over and over.

About a year later, Gramma was admitted to the State Mental Health Institute in Cherokee, Iowa. Commonly known as The Crazy House, it held criminals as well as the mentally ill. I can't help wondering now why Aunt Goldie opposed an Old Folks Home, but agreed to the mental hospital. I assume by that time there was no other alternative. They simply couldn't handle her.

Aunt Goldie and my mother, neither of whom could drive a car, relied on relatives to take them to visit Gramma, a 120 mile round-trip. Shortly before Christmas, 1954, Ma wrote to Billie:

Went to see Mama Sunday and I don't think she will last long. She doesn't know us at all, she seems almost like in a coma. don't even act like she can see us anymore. It has almost spoilt Christmas for me. I expect every day to hear she is gone, but you can't tell, she may be stronger than we think she is.

Agnes O'Brien Guertin died a few months later, on March 25, 1955, two months shy of being eighty-two-years-old. The cause of death was listed as a cerebral hemorrhage, cardiovascular disease, and senile brain disease with psychotic reactions.

Today, her illness is called Alzheimer's Disease. The symptoms are the same and, while there are medications and better care, there is no cure.

Alzheimer's might be unique in that the caregivers possibly suffer more than the patient. Those afflicted are unaware that they do not remember their loved ones; that they repeatedly ask the same questions. For the caregiver, there's still the question of what to do with Mother or Dad or a spouse, along with the guilt over putting a loved one in a facility. On the positive side, we've moved beyond the archaic practice of placing these patients in hospitals for the insane.

If Alzheimer's runs in families, my mother didn't live long enough to possibly be afflicted, but it struck her eldest daughter. Sybella always had a deep love for Gramma Guertin; in the end, they had this insidious disease in common.

Sybella was seventy-eight-years-old when she was moved from Sioux City to Yonkers, New York, to live with her son, Russ, his wife, Fran, and their three-year-old daughter, Shannon. The child and the woman bonded, enjoying a mutual admiration society that endured to the last.

When the time came to place Billie in a facility, her children and her siblings gave Russ total support. We were fortunate that one of the best homes in the country had an opening. St.

Cabrini Nursing Home in Dobbs Ferry, New York, has received a five star ranking by *U.S. News and World Report*. There, she was lovingly cared for by the staff, Russ, Fran, Shannon, and, at the end, by Hospice.

Russ recalls the experience as nine years of stress, but also as a time when, despite the distance of non-communication from his mother, he felt closer to her than he ever had. At Mass in the chapel, he watched with amazement when she sang along with familiar hymns. She loved music, and music seems to stay with us forever.

On Christmas, 2010, when she had been quiet for a long time, Russ asked, "What are you thinking about, Mom?"

With no hesitation she replied, "I miss my mom and dad." Her eyes were teary.

Long after Granny barely recognized Russ and Fran, her face lit up when Shannon appeared. Through their years together, Shannon read letters and cards to Granny, even when she no longer comprehended who had sent them.

Shannon remembers: *Since I was three-years-old, I have been [with] my grandma Billie. For the next four years, we loved doing arts and crafts on the kitchen table. We fed the birds from the back deck. The Alzheimer's got worse and worse, so eventually, she had to go live in Saint Cabrini Nursing home. She was moved when I was seven. I really missed doing the activities we did together, and it was really awkward when she wasn't there at home. On Sundays, my family would visit her and go to the Rose Room and play a game called Horse Racing. On March 10, 2012, I was with my grandma in her room (she was in bed) and she said, "Mama." It was the last and only word she said.*

Fran stayed the night with Billie, and the next morning, while Billie was awake and alert, Fran read a letter to her, written by Shannon. Later, after Russ arrived, Billie passed into the afterlife. She had once told her daughter, Jean, that she hoped to die on Good Friday, as our mother had. Instead, she died on our mother's birthday.

Jean had spent a week with her mother shortly before she died. Billie couldn't see well anymore, but when Jean entered the room the first day and spoke, Billie's face broke into a smile and her eyes filled with tears. She didn't call Jean by name during the week she spent there, but after Jean had gone, and Shannon came to visit, Billie called *her* Jean.

Jean's vigil beside her mother brought to mind a veiled memory from childhood, when she was just three-years-old (Shannon's age when she met her grandmother).

I am standing next to a bed that is pushed against a wall, and a window. I see a figure stretched out in front of me. I don't see a face, and when I look up, I see tree tops. It feels warm in the room, and I can hear my mother breathing. I hear my mother's soft voice saying something, but I don't understand it. I see long black hair lying along a flat body. I am amazed, and keep looking up and down the length of it. Then I am shuffled away.

Jean feels certain that the woman in bed was her great-grandmother, Agnes Guertin. As an adult, when Jean related this scene to her mother, Billie did not recall a particular visit to her grandma that might have generated the memory. But she confirmed that they did visit her several times at Aunt Goldie's house.

Ironically, one of Jean's first memories replayed itself more than fifty years later—only this time she was standing at her mother's bedside. She wonders if there was ever a time when her mother realized that she had the same illness that her grandmother had.

Sybella Reiners was buried on St. Patrick's Day, her favorite day of the year. Another connection to the Irish grandmother she loved.

Of Uncles And Aunts

I could tell you more.

~ ~ Cecelia Ann Dries

Adult relatives coming to visit held little interest for my siblings and me, unless there were cousins with whom we could play. Uncle Bill Dries and Aunt Alvina brought their children. Uncle Bill's mechanical hand—a hook—scared me, so I nodded a greeting to him and moved on to Aunt Alvina. "My, how you've grown," she always exclaimed. I smiled in response because she couldn't hear. She and Ma visited by passing a writing tablet back and forth on which they wrote comments.

When Poppy's bachelor brother, Bud, and spinster sister, Mayme, stopped by, we kids quickly disappeared. Poppy once described his youngest brother as naïve. My brother Joe told a story to illustrate the point. Uncle Bud was in a bar in Milwaukee when a woman sidled up to him and asked, "Hey, Bud, buy me a drink?"

Uncle Bud told Joe about the incident, adding, "I have no idea how she knew my name or why she thought I'd buy her a drink."

Uncle Bud and Aunt Mayme took frequent road trips to visit relatives and, once a year, a pilgrimage to the Grotto of the Redemption at West Bend. This group of religious grottos, constructed with rocks and precious stones, was designed by a German immigrant, Father Matthias Dobberstein, and built by him and two laborers. The story goes that as a seminarian, Dobberstein became gravely ill with pneumonia. He prayed to the Blessed Virgin to intercede and have his health restored. In turn, he would build a shrine in her honor. This year is its 100th anniversary.

A couple or three of us kids were invited along on trips to West Bend. It was probably a sin to say no to this religious experience, so we did our duty. It was about an hour and a half drive, and I can't imagine what we talked about with our aunt and uncle. Maybe we didn't; maybe they chatted in the front seat and we held court in the back. Probably snickering about them.

A trip with Uncle Bud and Aunt Mayme to Sioux City to visit Uncle Bill and Aunt Alvina and our cousins included a trek up Prospect Hill. At the top sat a monument built by Christian missionaries, and one had a view of the city, the Missouri River, and three states: Iowa, Nebraska, and South Dakota. No matter how many times Uncle Bud viewed the scene, it never failed to impress him.

Aunt Mayme's oddities were noticeable; her manner, her looks, her clothing, the whole picture. One day a neighbor girl and I were playing on her front porch when Aunt Mayme tottered by with her pigeon-toed gait. My friend giggled. "Look at that strange woman."

Aunt Mayme's tan cotton hosiery sagged on her bony legs, a shopping bag hung from one arm, a handbag from the other, and her hat bobbed precariously atop her mousy hair. I'd heard that she washed one side of her hair at a time so she didn't mess up the part. Wait—that was Aunt Cecelia, who had odd habits, too.

Aunt Mayme wore small round glasses and had chronic eczema on her face and arms. Her costume jewelry included large brooches, which she usually pinned on the shoulder of her dress instead of on the front. She had a butterfly shaped pin that she told me was made from human hair. Peeking at her dry gray hair, salted with dandruff, I couldn't imagine anyone making jewelry from that mess. One time I noticed her wearing only one earring and I told her she had lost an earring. She replied, "I know, but I always liked them so I still wear the one and people will think I just lost it."

I couldn't argue with the logic; that's what I'd assumed. I'd also seen her wear one dress atop another, maybe for warmth. I found it hard to believe she had gone to dressmaker's school and learned to design patterns and clothing, but that's what I'd been told.

On the day my friend and I saw her, she was headed for my house. Now and then she took the bus from Ashton to Sibley, to shop. She poked around downtown most of the day and then walked to our house, where Uncle Bud would come for her in the evening. At our house, she perched on a chair and rummaged in her shopping bag for several minutes and finally pulled out a package of cookies and what she called her common drinking cup. The tin cup collapsed into itself, but why she carried a water cup I don't know. If we had the weekly paper, she sat at the dining room table and read it word for word. Sometimes she nodded off, her head dropping to the table, which woke her.

One time she was alone in the dining room when the phone rang. She answered; someone asked for Shirley, and Aunt Mayme went to the stairs to call her. When Shirley came to the phone, she found the receiver in the cradle. Aunt Mayme had no phone and didn't know how to use one.

Ma once explained why Uncle Bud and Aunt Mayme had remained single. Uncle Bud was within days of getting married when his bride-to-be died after her appendix burst. She was buried in her wedding gown. As for Aunt Mayme, her parents had stepped between her and marriage because they believed her beau had his eye more on gaining access to the family farmland than on the supposed object of his affections. I found this story plausible. I'd seen pictures of Aunt Mayme as a young woman and she didn't come close to pretty, her face being more masculine than feminine. She lived at home and, after her mother died, she kept house for her father until he died. Then she moved into a little house in town and lived off her small inheritance and the kindness of relatives.

Aunt Cecelia, a former nun (discussed earlier), was also single. She taught school and lived independently, regularly snooping into the lives of her nieces and nephews and offering unsolicited advice on a variety of subjects.

When I chanced to think about their lost loves I felt sympathy, but that emotion failed to arise the day my friend poked fun at the strange woman. Like Judas denying Jesus, I did not acknowledge my aunt.

We kids always had the impression that Uncle Bud was rich. As a farmhand, and only himself to support, he surely had more money than Poppy had. Uncle Bud drove fairly new cars but never bought a new one. He took vacations to Chicago, Milwaukee, the Ozarks, and St. Louis. He owned the house we rented. He wore nice clothes and was well-groomed, if a bit heavy on the aftershave.

Later in life I knew more about Uncle Bud than I had as a child. He had been far from rich. A few days after he died, I received a letter from him postmarked the day he died. He asked for a loan of ten dollars. A couple of years earlier he'd requested a twenty dollar loan. In the 1940s, that would have been a substantial amount, but this was the 1980s and ten and twenty dollars didn't go far. I don't know why he needed those small amounts, but I'm glad he felt comfortable in asking me and that I could send it. I didn't send more than requested because I thought that might offend his pride. Although he'd probably laid pride aside when he wrote the letter. I never considered the money a loan; I didn't expect it back.

After his death, Aunt Cecelia wrote a tribute to her brother for the local paper. I learned that Uncle Bud had lived frugally all his life, enabling him to loan [give] money to friends and relatives. At age eighty, he had to rustle up odd jobs in his small hometown to supplement his meager Social Security checks. He undercharged for his handyman skills, especially when the people were elderly. He maintained cemetery plots and mowed lawns for family and friends, gratuitously.

Aunt Cecelia wrote, "Day by day one receives pleading letters from charitable organizations. Herman responded, over and over. You'd be surprised, as I was, at the amount he sent to starving people all over the world over his lifetime."

My family hadn't been starving, but we'd been on the receiving end of his thoughtfulness and generosity. He bought a house so that we'd have a place to live, and his yearly Christmas gift of apples is a treasured memory.

Today I remember Uncle Bud with respect and gratitude. I remember Aunt Mayme and Aunt Cecelia with affection—and, yes, humor.

Aunt Cel often ended a conversation or letter with the cryptic, "I could tell you more."

My brother Gary and I adopted this phrase as a mantra. We toss it at one another now and then.

I could tell you more.

Small Town Museum Holds Family History

Each of us needs a sense of where we belong.
In every family someone should take the
responsibility of becoming its historian.
Interview the old people; comb the attic,
then write up the information and circulate
it. When an old person dies it's like a library
burning. Don't let your library burn.

~ ~ Alex Haley, author

Most people, I suppose, cannot walk into a museum and find their family's past on display. It happened to me when I visited Brunson Heritage House in my hometown in Iowa.

Because the museum would be closed on the day I planned to be in Sibley, I had arranged a private tour. The Brunson Heritage House is a wing of the McCallum Museum, located in the park. The addition was opened in 1991 to hold an entire household of family memorabilia and antiques that had belonged to my cousin Dorthea Brunson.

Dorthea's maternal grandparents, Zebulon Eugene Guertin and his wife Mathilda, were my maternal great-grandparents. Parents of fifteen children, the Guertins emigrated to northwest Iowa from Canada in 1879. One of the daughters, Edna, was Dorthea's mother. One of the sons, Edgar, was my grandfather.

Dorthea, who never married, died in 1984. She bequeathed her house and its furnishings to the Osceola County Historical Society. Her parents, Edna and George Brunson, were charter members of the society when it was formed in 1936. Dorthea also left $60,000 for upkeep on her home, which she wanted open for public viewing. The society did this for several years, but it became difficult maintaining both the residence and the McCallum Museum. They did the next best thing; they sold Dorthea's house and built an addition to the museum to hold the entire household.

Before moving day, the committee took pictures of every room and made detailed lists of the location of every object. After the move, they tried to place each piece where it had been in the house. Adjustments had to be made because room sizes and wall space varied from the house.

The Brunson Heritage House was dedicated and opened to the public on June 15, 1991. The house is divided into a bedroom, parlor, and kitchen. The rooms look as inviting as Dorthea's home must have been. The kitchen is stocked with dishes and utensils from earlier eras, ready for preparing a family meal to be eaten around the oak table. In the bedroom, there's a ceiling high wooden wardrobe, and a huge, ornately carved oak bed made up with a quilt and plump pillows. The parlor has comfortable stuffed chairs with reading lamps beside them, and Dorthea's father's desk from when he taught country school in the early years of the 20th Century. On the walls are framed ancestral portraits. Other small photos and albums and hundreds of antiques are stored in display cases.

Not everything is family related. Dorthea collected antiques while she lived in California, where she worked as an interior designer. Also on display is her framed needlepoint, petit point, and tapestries. She created lamp shades and other objects from tin and copper, using the old pioneer craft of making designs by poking holes in the metal. Open for viewing are scrapbooks filled with souvenirs from Dorthea's 1920's school days.

I would like to have had the portraits and photos that were placed in the Brunson House, but that wasn't Dorthea's plan. I'm satisfied with her choice to see to it that family treasures did not fall into strangers' hands. Kept together in her Heritage House they are protected and preserved in this new century and beyond. Because of her legacy I can visit my family's past whenever I return to my hometown.

Kissing Cousins

A cousin is a ready-made friend for life.

~ ~ Unknown

Along with siblings, cousins are often our first playmates. I've always felt a strong connection to first cousins, even those I didn't know well. I had thirty first cousins by blood, and five from Aunt Sue's marriage to a widower with children.

In a black and white scene from early childhood, I watch my same age cousin tap dancing on a tabletop, her blonde curls bouncing, giving me jealousy pangs at the attention she's garnering. Bonnie wears black patent leather Mary Jane slippers and her white anklets have ruffles.

"Adorable. Another Shirley Temple," someone says.

Many years later, I discussed this memory with Uncle Jack Guertin. He said it was the day of his dad's funeral, at my grandparents' house after the burial. I would have been just four. I can't imagine now that I even knew who Shirley Temple was, but from the way her name was spoken I must have gleaned something magical about her.

No doubt about it, the adorable blonde movie moppet had the magic touch. And while my cousin conjured the Dimpled Temple, and had moved to California, I identified more with another young actress, Margaret O'Brien. Unlike

Princess Shirley in her frilly starched dresses and springy curls, Margaret was a commoner, like me. Dark-eyed, dark haired (often braided), gapped toothed, freckled, and wearing cotton dresses or overalls, she would have blended into my neighborhood. Shirley? Not so much.

Ma used to say that Margaret O'Brien and actor Pat O'Brien were her cousins, citing her mother's maiden name as proof. Although I eventually learned the relationship wasn't true, I liked to think of Margaret as a shirttail relative. I might have even boasted of it to friends. I *might* have.

Born Angela Maxine O'Brien on January 15, 1937 in San Diego, her first role lasted one minute, in *Babes On Broadway* (1941). Seems like hardly enough time to be noticed, but she caught the attention of producers and directors. Her first starring role was *Journey For Margaret* (1942), from which she adopted the name Margaret and made it legal. Her role as the bratty but beguiling Tootie in *Meet Me In St. Louis* (1944) won her an Academy Award as Outstanding Child Actress. After her Oscar was stolen by a household maid who fled town, the Academy replaced the statuette. Many years later, two antique dealers found the original award at a flea market and when they realized it was authentic, they returned it to O'Brien. I can't vouch for the truth of this story, but I read it somewhere.

I'm a sucker for a Margaret O'Brien film. Adept at laying on the drama, the child gave memorable performances in *Our Vines Have Tender Grapes* (1945), *Tenth Avenue Angel* (1948), *The Secret Garden* (1949), as Beth in *Little Women* (1949), and dozens of other films. Although the irresistible tyke became a money machine for MGM and she amassed a personal fortune, she did not fare well as an adolescent. She retired from the screen at the tender age of fourteen. Shirley Temple lasted until her early twenties before bowing out gracefully.

Both stars developed into dignified women who, if they made news, it was for something admirable. Temple dropped show business altogether and dabbled in politics. O'Brien had a quiet but steady career on television and on the dinner theater circuit. Married twice, she has one daughter. In 1996, she received the Women's International Center Living Legacy Award. In 2006, she received a Lifetime Achievement Award from the SunDeis Film Festival at Brandeis University. Today, she appears in the occasional television movie or program.

While many former child stars reminisce with negativity about those early years, O'Brien says she loved it. She concedes that Shirley Temple was a cut above other child actors of that era, but she claims for herself the title of Best Crier.

She illustrates her point with this story. When a director prompted her, at age six, to please gush some tears, she innocently asked, "Do you want the tears to run all the way down my cheeks or should I stop them halfway down?"

Now that's a pro. That's my cousin Margaret.

With A Song In Her Heart

*I love a piano, I love a piano, I love to hear
somebody play
Upon a piano, a grand piano, It simply carries
me away.*

~~ Irving Berlin

When I was a child in the 1940s, my family and the Foley family
lived in the same small town in Iowa. Aunt Goldie and Uncle
Elmer had eight children, and we had more than that, but for
every one of theirs, there was one of us the same age. We were
cousins and friends.

Five years my mother's senior, Aunt Goldie was my favorite
relative; a chatterbox and a gossip, with an Irish twinkle in her
eyes. When we visited the Foleys, someone eventually asked
Aunt Goldie to play the piano. It didn't take much urging; she
perched on the bench and we huddled around and harmonized
to the familiar tunes she plucked from the keyboard.

I once asked my mother "Why does Goldie know how to play
the piano and you don't?"

Ma explained, "Because when Mama gave us chores to do,
Goldie suddenly remembered her piano lessons. Mama let her
practice while the rest of us worked."

Pat Foley Sickelka, confirms my memory. "I was told that when she was younger, Grandma always volunteered to play the piano for everyone so she could get out of cleaning."

Jean Reiners Johnson relates her childhood memory of being in Great-aunt Goldie's kitchen. "I remember lots of laughter and her happy, smiling face. She was cute and feisty. Mom encouraged her to play the piano. I remember her walking towards it and it seemed like something important was about to happen! Then she played and people were singing, but I couldn't understand the words. I remember feeling happy. I wish I knew what song she played."

Goldie could tat and crochet, and late in life learned to drive a car, and my mother couldn't. Maybe big sister was practicing those skills, too, while Maybelle toiled.

Family lore has it that the piano was Goldie's first piece of furniture as a married woman, given to her in 1918 by her new husband before he went overseas to the world war. It's made by Strohber Piano Company, Chicago.

Decades later, JoAnn Klosterman Oster gained possession of the piano. She says, "Grandma gave me the piano when I was living in Sibley, about 1975. She wanted it close so she could play if the urge struck her. I refinished the piano; it had blackened with age and one of the sides had been damaged, so I replaced some of the wood with a walnut veneer. The thing I remember from before it was refinished is a round stain on the right side, where coffee cups probably sat. Grandma loved playing *Falling Waters*. Mom gave me the tattered piece of sheet music as a gift. She had framed it and encased it in glass to preserve what was left of a fragile piece of the past."

JoAnn's sister, Karen Teeselink, next in line to house the piano, says, "My best story about the piano is during one of our moves. The guys had loaded it on the back of a pickup. They turned out of the driveway and the piano fell off, stayed upright and rolled down the street. I didn't witness it, but my husband said it was hilarious, and a testament to the way they built pianos back then, that it survived intact. I personally think they wanted it to fall off because they were tired of moving it! When I told Mom the story, she laughed and said, "Grandma would be proud."

At a family event, Karen Teeselink asked if anyone would like to have Grandma's piano. Her cousin, Dawn Huisenga, quickly claimed it. Karen admitted that the piano had been in a shed for years and was not in great shape, but Dawn didn't care. She said, "I don't play the piano. I want it because it was Grandma's."

Now refinished and in Dawn's home, she covered the top with framed photos of Grandma Goldie and other family members. Dawn's favorite tune was *The Entertainer*, while others recall *Falling Waters*. The sheet music for *Falling Waters* is displayed. Dawn's father says, "Now if Dawn will only learn to play that piano."

Pat Sickelka says, "I remember watching Grandma's fingers fly over the keys. She always had a huge smile on her face! Without doubt, *Falling Waters* was her masterpiece!"

On a family Facebook page Becky Foley wrote, "I remember that Grandma toured Liberace's house and got to play his piano."

Becky's sister, Mary Palmer, added, "I remember watching Lawrence Welk with Grandma and her telling us that she danced with him, and with Don Ho in Hawaii."

Grandson Todd Windes made a recording of her playing the piano. The quality is poor, but Suzyn Foley Purdy wrote, "More than the music it brought me to tears just hearing her talk."

Karen Teeselink added, "I had forgotten how much I loved the deep tone of that piano. When I was a child we had a 'modern' piano and there is such a difference in sound."

Now, after almost a hundred years, a tangible piece of family history has another home. Maybe someone will learn to play, and *Falling Waters* will once again be heard when the family gathers.

{ PIECE WORK }

The Fame Of The Name

Certain shades of limelight wreck a girl's complexion.

~ ~ Truman Capote, *Breakfast At Tiffany's*

When I left home for the first time, my new friends and co-workers called me Donna. I had a sister-in-law Donna so it became confusing; we were both Donna Dries. My family still called me Madonna. When I married, I became Donna Christensen to my in-laws and newly-made friends, but my family still called me Madonna. My first published work had the byline Donna Christensen, but I learned that there was another writer in town with that name. Someone mentioned seeing an article I'd written but it didn't sound like me. It wasn't mine. I cleared up the mess. I decided that Madonna was a more distinctive byline, so I chose my given name/maiden name/married name. My family by marriage and some friends still call me Donna.

I've known only four others with the name Madonna: an older cousin; a girl my brother dated; the sister of a guy I dated, and our namesake, the Blessed Lady. She's the one a librarian was referring to when she handed back my card and said, "Pretty name. Is it hard to live up to?"

I replied that I had never tried living up to it.

That was before the infamous Madonna, the celebrity. Once her name became a household word, it's been a case of *living it down.*

A doctor, studying my chart, said, "Madonna, huh? Well, I don't think the other one has any talent and I'm sure you're nicer than she is."

Now that's bedside manner.

When my daughter told her college friends that her mother's name was Madonna, they scoffed, "Yeah, right." She showed them my return address label.

At a family reunion, my young nieces giggled that they couldn't wait to tell their friends they had been with Madonna over the weekend.

Sometimes when store clerks scan my credit card they glance at me, checking to see if it could possibly be ... One look clears that up. I would never be mistaken for the music star. I'm older, I wear glasses, I have dark hair (she does, too, sometimes), and I never wear a metal bra. In Florida's heat and humidity?

One young bank teller said, "Wow, you have a famous name. I've never met a Madonna."

"I had the name before she did," I said.

She smiled. "She used to be my idol."

"Not anymore?"

"Nah, I've grown up."

Behind me in line, a woman said, "I heard Madonna's gonna have a baby, but I've never heard who the father is."

"Maybe a virgin birth," I offered.

A journalist who interviewed me for an article said, "Maybe it's because I'm a child of the eighties, but I think your name is awesome."

More recently, a technician about to take my bone density test said with a laugh, "Your name. I love it. I was excited when I saw the name Madonna on your chart."

The other Madonna has invaded my writing territory, too, on the Internet. But she writes children's books so I don't have to compete with her there. However, I often end up in the same search engine hits, where some of them offer nude photos of the other one. Because of the name connection and the title of my first book, *Swinging Sisters* has shown up on porn sites. Let the buyer beware; the content is a far cry from what the title might suggest.

Someone once told me she can't stand Madonna, but she admires her business savvy and the way she promotes herself. I do not admire her for any reason.

Her latest promotional gimmick, an ad for her new perfume, Truth Or Dare, had network executives pondering if it was too racy for prime time. Far be it from me to defend Madonna, but I had to laugh; I didn't think anything today was too racy for prime time, and, have we not seen Madonna's cleavage and her sexy antics before? I believe we have.

I understand that the former Catholic now adheres to Kabbalah, a faith based on the study of Hebrew texts. And she changed her name to Esther.

All you Esthers of the world—prepare yourselves. Should Madonna's new name become ingrained in public consciousness, bear with it and hope she changes her name again.

Collected Scents

In the darkened garden, lit only by pagoda lights
And fireflies a'glitter, a marmalade cat
Prowled the flagstone path.
Wind chimes tinkled a merry tune,
And nocturnal life conversed in the trees.

From the flower bed nearby, a fragrance wafted to me;
Out of the past, familiar,
But the perfume had no name
Until my husband, the gardener, asked,
"Do you smell the four o'clocks?"

Swiftly I was carried back to childhood,
To a window box filled with rich Iowa soil
Nurturing petunias, morning glorys, and four o'clocks,
Whose potpourri entered our house
Through screened, lace-curtained windows.

That lusty essence, now renewed,
Evokes an image dear, of quiet summer evenings;
My mother at her window box, while I, unknowingly,
Collected scents that would pass through time,
Linking me with yesterday.

Notions About Neighbors

Hey, Boo.

~ ~ Scout Finch in *To Kill A*
Mockingbird, Harper Lee, 1962

Children are adept at conjuring tales about folks who seem *different*. In small towns these people are visible to young eyes and vulnerable to imagination. Think witches, spies, and ghosts. Think Harper Lee's Boo Radley.

Mrs. Drake, across the street from one of our early houses, wore long black dresses and a black shawl; her gray hair was straggly; she had whiskers on her chin; she kept a houseful of cats (familiars?), and she carried a cane. She might as well have had *Witch* stamped on her forehead like a scarlet A.

Next door to us, George Trostle scanned the sky with a telescope, while in the house his short wave radio sputtered and crackled with static and broken voices, some of them German—we were pretty sure. Conclusion: He was a spy for the enemy; his cover being a volunteer fireman and, during the war, an air raid warden.

At the Ninth Street house, in the dark of night, we often heard an eerie wail, "Rubeee, Rubeee." Ma said it was an elderly invalid woman calling to her daughter, Ruby, who took care of her. We'd never seen the patient, so we fancied that it might be her ghost calling.

A block south, along the railroad track, lived a woman we called Crazy Margaret. If we dared come anywhere near her shack, she emerged and chased us with a broom. Another witch? Of course.

Outside the neighborhood, we encountered other *strange* folks, among them a man we kids called by his last name: Campbell. He bided his time on the steps by Brunson Hardware, talking to himself. He was later committed to the state hospital for the insane.

One man, whose name we never knew, showed up downtown on Saturday nights. It's the only time I ever saw him. Tall and thin, with a sharp nose, and eyes that seemed to pop out of his head, he stood on a corner, hands crossed in front at his waist, and watched people, mostly young girls, or so Shirley and I thought. Sometimes he loped down the street, arms dangling, shoulders and head thrust forward, his head cranking sideways, his eyes darting from side to side. Shirley and I ducked into a store if we saw him coming.

Lynn Glover, a familiar figure, endeared himself to adults and kids. We called him Glover. His father, one of Sibley's first settlers, had at various times been a minister, a lawyer, a judge, and mayor. Lynn had been well-educated, but had bypassed a white collar career. He was not a bum, nor was he homeless. He supported himself as a day laborer: brick mason, plasterer, wallpaper hanger, carpenter—he could handle the job. He worked for a low wage, sometimes only a meal for a small job. His *office* was on the bank corner or the steps by Brunson Hardware (beside Campbell). Glover slept above the post office in a room said to be no bigger than a closet. He wore tattered clothing, sometimes layers of garments, and a hat pulled over his long gray hair. He shuffled his feet, perhaps to keep his worn, untied shoes from falling off.

He toted the tools of his trade in a two-wheeled handcart. One day he shuffled into our backyard and we watched, fascinated, as he vanished into the cistern to reline it. From time to time we called to him, to hear our echo.

"Do you need any of your tools?"

"Are you okay?"

His replies echoed back. He was fine; didn't need anything.

At noon, we reported to him that Ma had brought out a plate of food. He climbed out of the darkness and sat under the apple tree to eat. Inside, we gobbled our food and then hurried outside so as not to miss a minute of being up close and personal with Glover.

He took some of his meals at the Palace Café. Ma said he loved ice cream and he ate dessert first, while waiting for his meal. Uncle Jack Guertin told this story about Glover. One time Jack's wife, Maude, and their young daughter, Patty, went into the Palace and sat down at the counter. Patty wanted a piece of watermelon and the waitress said they were all out; she had just taken an order for the man a few stools away. Glover overheard the talk and when his watermelon came, he passed the plate to Patty and ordered something else.

Glover had inherited some of his father's possessions, including a vintage car. At one time he stored these materials in Enright's garage. On rainy days, we kids crowded into the car and leafed through musty smelling law books and papers, speculating on why Glover had chosen to live the way he did.

It remains a mystery.

In one case, our speculation concerned both a person and her house along the boulevard, its windows always covered with dark green window shades. The place belonged to Hattie Lindaman, a middle-aged spinster with cropped white hair, a sturdy build, and fairly tall for a woman. When she gardened and did yard work in the summer she wore cotton dresses, black oxfords, white anklets, and a sunbonnet. When she walked to town to conduct business, she chose a wide-brimmed straw hat and carried a basket over her arm. In winter, she dressed in a black coat, black hat, and dark stockings.

So—nothing unusual about Hattie's appearance. Nor did our interest have anything to do with the fact that her house sat in close proximity to the funeral home, where unimaginable procedures took place and who knew how many bodies were lying about. What set Hattie apart and captured our attention was that she kept a whale in her basement.

Absurd?

What do you mean? It was a fact.

Once, when Shirley and I saw Hattie leave, we waited until she was out of sight and then we circled the house, trying to see inside the basement, but the windows were covered like those on the house. It wasn't so much that we needed evidence; we wanted a look at the dreaded captive creature.

Fast forward to 1983. I no longer lived in Sibley but I subscribed to the weekly newspaper. I saw an article about an artist, Patsy Q. Bailey, who was showing her work at the library. Among the paintings pictured was a watercolor called Spinster's House. I knew it as The Whale Lady's House. I wrote to Ms. Bailey and asked about buying the painting. She said it was sold but that she could do another rendition for me. I commissioned her to do so.

When I explained my interest in the house (and the fantasy we kids had), Bailey told me that she had long been fascinated with the house and decided to paint it when she saw it in the purple light of early morning. She chose a faded yellow for the house, to represent warm family memories. She painted the sky purple, as she'd seen it, and to represent sadness that Hattie had never married, and that her life, and the life of the house, was nearly over.

Bailey added that while she was painting the original, Hattie's niece was taking drawing lessons from her. One day the woman asked if the painting could be removed from the room. She said the picture gave her the creeps.

To me, the painting represents childhood. Hanging in my office, the scene captures the derelict charm of the once elegant home, a stately specter at once rising silently out of the shadows and crumbling into its foundation

Through Bailey's information and *Gazette* articles, I pieced together Hattie's story. The land where the house stood was granted from the United States Government to the State of Iowa in 1873. In 1877, it was granted to the Sioux City and St. Paul Railroad, which granted it to the Iowa Land Company in 1881.

The first private owner was W. H. Armin who, in 1892, built what was considered by many the finest home along the Ninth Street boulevard. He didn't choose the popular Victorian style with a wraparound porch; instead, the house was a boxy structure with a mansard roof and more than a dozen windows across the front, including those in the enclosed porch entry. The back also had an enclosed porch entry. The spacious house had three bedrooms, a bath, and walk-in closets on the upper floor. The first floor had a parlor, living room, dining room, one bedroom, and a kitchen.

In 1906, John Lindaman, a carpenter, bought the house and he and his wife, Tillie, moved in with three children. The oldest, William, later married and moved to a nearby town where he served as Postmaster until his death. The second son, Pearl, died at age thirty-two. Hattie, who was twelve when she came to the house, graduated from the high school up the street and, in her early life was active in the First Presbyterian Church. She remained living at home, and cared for her parents as they aged.

After their deaths in the 1940s, Hattie drew the shades in their downstairs bedroom, closed the door, and left things as they were. As time progressed, she closed room after room, eventually living and sleeping in the kitchen. She allowed no one to enter the house. Day and night, the shades remained pulled to the sill.

Hattie kept her yard and garden immaculate and, over the years, tried to keep the house from deteriorating. It was difficult to keep the flat roof repaired, and rain caused considerable damage. The furnace blew up once, causing smoke damage to the closed rooms. In the painting I have, there is an oil barrel by the back door, so she evidentially gave up on the furnace and heated the one room she used with an oil stove.

Hattie suffered a broken hip in 1980 and was moved to a nursing home. Her niece, who became conservator of the property, honored Hattie's wish that no one be allowed in the house.

Sometime later, I saw in the paper a notice of auction of the real estate and household goods of Hattie Lindaman. The list of items evidenced that time had stood still for her: A treadle sewing machine, a wringer washer, a kerosene stove, a horse robe, a pedal grindstone, a player piano with a cabinet full of rolls, a fainting couch with claw feet and a lion's head on each side, brass beds, a high-backed oak bed, many other pieces of oak furniture, quilts, trunks, and a reel-type lawnmower that I'd seen her use many times. The only concessions to progress were a refrigerator and a gas stove.

The property was purchased by a man who was interested only in the materials inside the home: the woodwork, doors, mantels, and stair bannister, all of which he sold to a man who was renovating a home of the same vintage. The buyer then sold the property to a couple who were interested only in the prime location on which the house stood.

The April 26, 1984 issue of the *Gazette* carried a picture of Hattie's house, with the announcement that it was scheduled to be burned as an exercise by the fire department. A later paper carried a picture of the house in flames, smoke pouring out the windows and doors.

I like to think that Hattie wasn't told about this event, that she was safe from the world she shunned, remembering that she once lived in one of the grandest homes in town.

Hattie died in 1996, at age one hundred and one. In her obituary, along with the usual details, were these words: *Throughout her life, Hattie maintained her independence, both in her style of living and in her relations with others. She took care of her home and finances as long as she could.*

Hattie could never have imagined that a little girl who lived down the street and had strange ideas about her, remembered her and has a painting of her house hanging on the wall.

And the girl, now a woman, has written a story about The Whale Lady, and included it in a book of memoirs.

Please Favour With Your Autograph

*I stopped believing in Santa Claus when
Mother took me to a department store to see
him and he asked for my autograph.*

~ ~ Shirley Temple

Celebrity autographs bring high prices on the collectibles market, but the autograph books used by children in the early part of the last century are priceless. Popular as birthday or Christmas gifts, kids passed these books around toward the end of the school year, exchanging simple verses about friendship.

The books from my era had pastel pages of yellow, pink, green, and blue. Friends picked a favorite color on which to write, or an appropriate color (blue) for: *I hope your life is never the color of this page.* Some chose the inside covers so they could write this verse: *By hook or by crook, I'll be the first [or last] to write in your book.* Another favorite called for turning the book upside down: *When you look upon this page and frown, remember the girl who wrote her name upside down.*

From what I recall, collecting autographs was more popular with girls than with boys. If boys did write a message they tended to be brief and they avoided anything hinting at lovey-dovey. They used the generic *Best wishes*, or, *To a swell pal.* If boys wrote a complete verse it was often silly: *Way down south, where the bananas grow, an ant stepped on an elephant's toe.* Or good-natured sarcasm: *Don't worry; the Liberty Bell is cracked, too.* And: *Two, four, six, eight, they'll never let you graduate.*

Among teenagers, love and marriage were common subjects. *Don't kiss the boys by the garden gate; love is blind, but the neighbors ain't. First comes love, then comes marriage, then comes Dora with a baby carriage.*

This risqué verse might cause a young girl to blush if a boy were so bold as to write: *I love you little, I love you mighty, I love your pajamas next to my nightie. Now don't get excited, and don't be misled; I mean on the clothesline, not in bed.*

In my small collection of autograph books, I have three representing three generations of one family, William Amos Lord, his daughter, Ethel, and her daughter, Evelyn. The inscription on the first page of eight-year-old Evelyn's brown leather book reads: To Evelyn from Virginia, Xmas, 1926. On the inside cover, Evelyn wrote: Do not tear out any pages. Ethel's book has the same request. They obviously wanted no censoring. A boy couldn't write something mushy and then change his mind and get rid of the evidence by tearing out the sheet.

The verses in Evelyn's book were written between January 1927 and June 1933. Some of the same rhymes appear in her mother's childhood book. Like jump rope songs, autograph verses were handed down from one generation to the next.

William Lord wrote in Evelyn's book in June, 1930: *To my darling granddaughter Evelyn. May your life be long and happy, may the future e'er be bright. May thy wishes all be granted, and thy cares be few and light. Your loving grandpa, Wm. Amos Lord.* Evelyn's sister and parents wrote verses following his.

Evelyn's mother, Ethel, was ten and lived in San Francisco when she collected autographs from 1900-1903. The front cover of her book is ivory celluloid on which is a landscape scene. The back cover is burgundy velvet. The first page has a drawing of a table, on which sits a vase with flowers laid beside it. The person who drew the picture and wrote the verse, Kingsley Cannon, took the time to use script resembling calligraphy. *Dear Ethel: We judge ourselves by what we feel capable of doing, while others judge us by what we have done.*

It appears from the maturity of the verse and drawing that Kingsley Cannon was an adult. He used black ink, whereas most of the children wrote in pencil and their faded verses are no longer legible. Perhaps he was a friend of the family and had given the book to Ethel for her birthday or another occasion.

Ethel's mother wrote: *My darling daughter Ethel. Be a good girl and may God bless you and keep you always is the earnest wish and prayer of your loving mother, Mary L. Lord.*

Silly signoffs were common in both books. *Yours until Goat Island has kids. Yours until the kitchen sinks. Yours until elephants roost in trees. Yours until the Mississippi wears rubber pants to keep her bottom dry.* A boy named Mickey folded a page into the spine of Evelyn's book and wrote, *If you are beautiful, open this.* Of course, Evelyn would have opened it, to find that Mickey had chided her with the words, *Stuck Up!*

William Lord's book from 1873 is a bit different; it appears to be a form of parlor game for adults. Printed in gold on the green cover are the words: *Mental Photographs.* Inside the cover: *This is An Album For Confessions of Taste, Habits, and Convictions.* The owner signed his name, William A. Lord, and added: *Please favour with your autograph. Nosce Te ipsum* (know thyself).

Each person using the book had two pages on which there were forty questions to answer, among them: Your favorite color, flower, tree, gem, season, names, musicians, writers, books ... The preface explains that answers may be in jest or earnest, as best suits the mind and manner of the person responding. The idea was to form a mental picture of the person from the answers given. A photograph could be added, but only one young woman pasted her photo in the album. In response to the question: *What are the saddest words*, several people answered: *It might have been.* Among choices for the sweetest words: *Mother, Home, Thank you, Dear,* and, *Come to dinner.*

Another question asked: *What is your idea of misery?* Answers: *Toothache, tight boots, poverty, nothing to do.* And: *What character trait do you admire most in a man? Humor, honesty, manliness, honor, pluck, and bravery* were popular choices. For women: *womanliness, modesty, faith, virtue, gentleness, and talkativeness.* One chap confessed the trait he most admired in women was nudity. Responding to: *What do you believe to be your most distinguishing characteristics,* one woman wrote: *Ugliness and Ignorance.* I wonder if that was written in jest or in earnest.

Open a vintage autograph book and you'll see a repository for legible, cursive penmanship, an art that is slowly being lost.

Here's to auld acquaintance, of memories fond and dear. Pleasant times in bygone days, Good health, Good luck, Good cheer.

Yours until Niagara Falls, your affectionate friend, Abigail.

Autograph Books Revisited

Every job is a self-portrait of the person who does it. Autograph your work with excellence.

~ ~ Unknown

Three years after my article about autograph books appeared in *Yesterday's Magazette*, the publisher, Ned Burke, received an e-mail from a reader, Leesa Cannon.

Leesa wrote that she found the story while using Google to research her great-grandfather, Kingsley Cannon, of San Francisco. He was a lawyer, who adopted a son and named him Kingsley W. Cannon, Jr. Leesa's father is Kingsley W. Cannon III. Leesa wrote, "Thanks for the familial clue."

The story might have ended there, but as a genealogist, I know the value of such clues. Since I had no family connection to this particular book, I responded to Leesa and offered to send her the book. She was delighted and, on receiving it, commented:

> Thank you for your generosity. Aside from the obvious family interest, it's an amazing piece of history. I know that these sayings are passed down through generations; therefore, when asked to sign someone's book, I plan to use my great-grandfather's quote. It's also interesting

to see the similarity between the written name in the corner and my father's handwriting. But my dad is funny. He said, 'How do I know it's him?' But I find it valuable, even if he does not.

More than one hundred years ago, Kingsley Cannon sketched a picture and penned a verse to a little girl. She kept the autograph book in which it was written, and her daughter later kept the book. Neither would have imagined that one day, through an electronic conduit, the book and the verse would be returned to and treasured by the great-granddaughter of the man who wrote it.

This story was published in *Family Tree Magazine*'s Everything's Relative column, May/June 2012.

Little Dairy On The Prairie

My father was a milkman. So, I, too, delivered milk.

~ ~ Karl Malden

All roads led to Sibley, the county seat for Osceola County. Along with the courthouse, the principal hub of activity was the Osceola Co-op Creamery, the town's largest employer.

A typical production day began at the scores of outlying farms. Up before dawn, farmers carrying lanterns headed for darkened barns to attend dairy cows lowing to be relieved. As the sun rose, the country roads burst with activity as route drivers picked up the five or ten gallon cans of fresh milk set out by farmers. For each full can retrieved, the driver left an empty can for use the next morning.

Back at the creamery, the drivers dumped their milk at the receiving room, where it was weighed and tested for butterfat. The men kept records of where the milk came from and its weight and butterfat content, so farmers could be paid accordingly. The drivers washed and sterilized the cans they'd emptied and then loaded them back on the truck for the next day. After completing this, some drivers had a second job at the creamery or elsewhere. Others delivered milk, butter, and cheese to stores and homes. If bottles of milk were left on the doorstep too long in the winter, the cream that had risen to the top froze into a yellowish cube and pushed itself through the paper cover on the bottle.

My brother recalls that for a while in the 1940s, after Poppy had his heart attack, he drove a milk route for a man who temporarily couldn't drive for some reason, but was able to handle the heavy work. One man helping the other.

Young boys often earned their first pocket money riding shotgun on a father's or older brother's milk route, hefting the filled cans in and out of the truck. Milk built muscles in more ways than one.

In addition to handling tons of milk, the creamery produced cheese, butter, and ice cream. The cheese and butter were sold by local grocers and also shipped wholesale in bulk to retailers who put their own brand name on it. The same happened with ice cream, shipped in bulk, except none was sold retail locally. However, if you stopped by the creamery office, you could purchase a cone filled with fresh, rich ice cream.

The ice cream shop in town, owned by Jack Lyons and his wife, whose name I've forgotten, sold Worthmore ice cream, produced in Worthington, Minnesota. Its logo read: Eat All You Want—It's Good For You. No lie; it was tasty. Cherry Nut and Almond Fudge were my favorites.

To recognize the co-op efforts of the creamery, its employees, and the farmers, Sibley held an annual Creamery Day. It fell during the winter when farmers had time to spend a day in town. Everyone turned out for the event: farmers and their wives, creamery employees, route drivers, businessmen, working men and women from other businesses, retired folks, housewives, and school kids.

For kids, the day might be frigid, or icy, or rainy, but come deep snow or high water, we wouldn't miss the event. Instead of going home at noon, we hustled off to the Legion Hall. There we joined the throng, standing in line to pick up a free cheese sandwich in a buttered bun, a bottle of chocolate milk, and a paper cup of ice cream. Coffee and doughnuts were available all day, as long as the affair lasted.

Today, there is no creamery in Sibley. Smaller enterprises keep the town going. There are currently about 2800 residents, roughly the same as when I lived there.

I can't help wondering if there's anything to match the excitement and community involvement of Creamery Day, with a bonus of free lunch.

Come to think of it, there's fun to be had at Max Theaters. In addition to running the latest movies, they hold Bowl Night (bring your own bowl and have it filled with popcorn for a dollar); Dollar Night (popcorn and soda each a dollar); and Pizza Night (order before the movie and have it delivered from Pizza Ranch).

One County's Greatest Generation

*It is, I believe, the greatest generation any
society has ever produced.
These men and women fought not for fame
and recognition, but because it was the right
thing to do. When they came back they rebuilt
America into a superpower.*

~ ~ Tom Brokaw, *The Greatest
Generation*, 1998.

Osceola County, Iowa, occupies only 397 square miles in
the northwest corner of the state. In 1942, like towns and
cities across the country, this agricultural community sent its
youngsters to fight a war in lands they never expected to see.
Barely more than children, they parked the tractor or rose
from their school desks and headed for the enlistment office.
As green as field corn, they joined friends who'd been stocking
shelves at the grocery, pumping gas at the filling station,
working as secretaries, or plugging a probe into a slot at the
telephone office and asking "Number, please?" Some were in
college; others handed over their law or medical practice to
caretakers and signed on for an unknown duration. An earlier
generation of men who once believed they'd fought the war to
end all wars squared their shoulders and held back tears as

they put sons and daughters aboard trains and waved them out of sight.

As the war accelerated, Mrs. George Rehms began clipping from the weekly paper any news related to these young people. She and her husband had two sons in the service. The clippings ranged in size from two inch items about a serviceman home on furlough to a long account from a soldier who spent three terrible years in a prison camp in Manchuria after being captured at Bataan. Reverend Leo Berger's eloquent eulogy at President Roosevelt's memorial service joined reports of Bronze Stars, Silver Stars, Purple Hearts, and too many headlines reading: Killed In Action.

The letter-writers rarely complained, and often advised Mom not to worry. The most requested items were letters, cigarettes, candy, and socks. Bursting with what might have been false bravado, J.E., later wounded and awarded a Purple Heart, wrote:

> Sometimes I have to get down in the foxhole as the Germans try and lob a few artillery shells. We've got about all the snipers cleaned out of this area now. The boys don't have much love for snipers. When we locate their position they come out with their hands in the air yelling "comrad." Well, they don't want to come yelling comrad at me. A person can't take any chance with them. I don't believe in taking prisoners.

During one period, thirteen members of the medical unit of the Iowa National Guard were missing in action in North Africa. They were later found in German and Italian prison camps. Letters from the men kept townsfolk covertly updated on their whereabouts, condition and, finally, their release.

Photos in the paper told their own stories: A woman seated next to pictures of her seven sons in uniform. J.C. Penney's display windows filled with pictures of men in uniform. A smiling, youthful airman beside a headline announcing he'd been killed in England. On the day word reached his parents, they received a letter from him saying that he was okay and that Christmas packages were coming through.

Near the end of the war, the woman collecting the clippings received this letter:

Dear Mrs. Rehms:

Recently your son, Technical Sergeant Elmer L. Rehms, was decorated with the Air Medal. It was an award in recognition of courageous service to his combat organization, his fellow American airmen, his country, his home, and you. He was cited for meritorious achievement while participating in aerial flights in the Pacific from December 10, 1944 to April 2, 1945. Your son took part in sustained operational flight missions during which hostile contact was probable and expected. These flights aided considerably in the recent successes in the theatre. Almost every hour of every day your son, and the sons of other American mothers, are doing just such things as that here in the Pacific. Theirs is a real and tangible contribution to victory and to peace. I would like to tell you how genuinely proud I am to have men such as your son in my command, and how gratified I am to know that young Americans with such courage and resourcefulness are fighting our country's battles against the Japanese aggressors. You, Mrs. Rehms, have every reason to share that pride and gratification.

Sincerely, George C. Kennedy,

General, United States Army, Commanding.

Another Osceola County man, George Braaksma, returned home from the war and began farming; he and his wife raised nine children. In 1983, he bought Mrs. Rehms's two to three thousand newspaper clippings at her household auction. He painstakingly glued the pieces chronologically into a scrapbook. He offered to let people stop by his house to see the collection. Interest ran high, and the local printing company produced a short run of copies. They sold out, as did a second printing.

This limited edition book is unpretentious; reproduced the way Braaksma created it, 140 pages, spiral bound and about the size of a U.S. road atlas. Its content, however, circles the globe.

Newspaper Clippings of Osceola County WW II Veterans could be the most thorough record of one county's participation in any war. Knock on any door across America during World War II and you'd find someone touched by the battles raging across Africa, Europe, and Asia. But it's unlikely that another collection like Mrs. Rehms's, preserved in Braaksma's scrapbook, would have been found.

The letters used in this article were written long before political correctness became a part of our language. Altering the text to conform to today's standards would tamper with their authenticity. I also did not edit spelling. I donated a copy of this scrapbook to the library at the World War II Museum in New Orleans.

This story was published in Silver Boomer Books' anthology: *The Harsh And The Heart: Celebrating The Military.*

To give credit where credit is due—after writing this article I learned that Emma Engelkes also kept a scrapbook like Braaksma's. A few copies were made and were sold through the museum and the historical society.

The Lone Wolf

*For the strength of the pack is the wolf, and
the strength of the wolf is the pack.*

~ ~ Rudyard Kipling

My parents had a print of The Lone Wolf prominently displayed
in all the houses we lived in from the 1920s-1950s. I don't
know when or where they acquired the artwork; I know its
provenance only since they departed this world. My oldest
brother took possession and then one of his daughters.

The original painting, The Lone Wolf, is by Alfred von
Wierusz-Kowalski (1849)1915). Born in Poland, the artist studied
in Warsaw and Dresden before entering Munich Academy of
Fine Arts and settling in Munich. His work won numerous
awards and was sought after by private collectors as well as art
dealers in Germany and the United States. In 1890 Kowalski
became an honorary professor of the Munich Academy. His
paintings are now found in Polish museums.

Kowalski's body of work is impressive, stunning detailed
images of European peasantry in the late 1800s. An Internet
source reports that the artist's family had once been attacked
by wolves. That sounds plausible, for wolves are common in
his paintings: Lone wolves, wolves in packs, wolves pursuing
or attacking men and horses. Many of the paintings are

wintertime, with snow and ice and horse-drawn sleighs in bleak landscapes.

One of the most popular home decorating items of the early 20th Century, the ubiquitous print came in different views; the wolf faced right, or sometimes left. When listed on eBay, sellers call the buildings a camp, a ranch, or a village. The least common of the prints shows mountains in the background, a lake or river, and the buildings. Some show a single building.

In a discussion board on the Internet, anonymous writers speculated on the meaning behind The Lone Wolf.

The austere and cold imagery is an illustration of the coldness of the world ... one not connected to God or his fellowman. Subconsciously, ignorantly, or willfully we choose to live in a way that leaves us out in the cold.

An image of the darkness of man's soul.

Meant to portray one's strength during solitude and change.

He speaks to our soul and to those who do not understand that all beings, even the most savage, are entitled to acceptance, compassion, and purpose.

The wolf may be a father, or a mother. Neither is afraid of death, for it is inevitable, but mindful and most intelligently watchful of what is and what has been already.

A symbol of hope.

One obvious theme is the harshness of winter and the survival drive of the wolf.

Are the cabins symbolic of the intrusion of humans into the wolf's territory, and the impending end of the wolf's rule?

One could repeatedly guess about the artist's intent. He obviously had a connection to wolves. For me, the scene is peaceful, reminiscent of Christmas—of *Silent Night, all is calm, all is bright.* The picture is a comfortable link to the past; to a quiet rural life in the Midwest, where The Lone Wolf graced our parlor wall.

Books As Memorials

There is not such a cradle of democracy upon the earth as the Free Public Library, this republic of letters, where neither rank, office, nor wealth receives the slightest consideration.

~ ~ Andrew Carnegie

In this digital age there is much speculation about the future of printed books. Although the day might come when books are no longer published as we know them, I believe that books will long be revered and safely held in libraries, museums, in private collections, and in homes around the world. Bound books will be tangible proof that our way of life existed, that we were here for a spell and left a message.

As a child frequenting my hometown library in Iowa, it would not have occurred to me that someday there would be books on these shelves with my name as author. But it was there I developed a love for reading, for the feel of a book in my hands, for the smell of printers ink and paste, for the construction and artistry, from an enticing cover to a synopsis about what to expect from the story, an author's photo and bio, and, in some cases, colorful illustrations. My books are now shelved in the Iowa Room of Sibley Public Library, and I have an open invitation to stop by for an author Meet and Greet book signing.

Much to my surprise, I recently found a Google entry showing that two of my books were on the Memorial Shelf at the T.B. Scott Free Library in Merrill, Wisconsin. I don't know anyone in Merrill; I have no connection to the small town, although my German and Irish ancestors emigrated to Wisconsin and I have family still there. Naturally, I was curious about why my books were on the Memorial Shelf. I e-mailed the librarian, asking if he could tell me who made the donation and in whose memory.

Donald Litzer replied, "The answer to your question is: Not yet!"

He explained that the Memorial Shelf contains books and audio-videos that donors may purchase for a special occasion, in memory of or in honor of someone. The gift often represents a particular interest of the honoree. When a gift is purchased, a personalized bookplate is added and the item goes into general circulation.

The items offered for sale as memorials are selected by a librarian assistant, sometimes personal choices; others that are recommended by staff members. Memories and nostalgia are considered good topics, and Mr. Litzer believes that my books, *Toys Remembered* and *Dolls Remembered*, were chosen for that reason.

Statistics vary on how many books are published in a given year—multi-thousands, to be sure. I'm honored that my anthologies were selected by T.B. Scott Free Library. I have since donated another of my books, *Swinging Sisters*.

The library's Website captures the spirit and value of their unique endowment and gift program: *Libraries hold the wealth of the world. They allow free access to the accumulated thoughts of many cultures. They open their doors to all of us; they connect us to one another. Gifts to libraries are a time-honored way of contributing to the quality of life of the community, and by extension, the world at large. When we give a gift to our community library, we affirm the people and the places that hold meaning and promise for us. We leave a legacy for the enrichment of this and future generations.*

Underneath It All

*In olden days a glimpse of stocking was
looked upon as shocking, now Heaven knows,
anything goes.*

~ ~ Cole Porter

Undergarments. Underwear. Underpants. Unmentionables, they were once called. Today, there's nothing unmentionable about them, nor are some of them even *under*. Victoria has no secrets.

Bra straps showing, once a tacky wardrobe malfunction, are now a fashion statement. Not only the straps. Singer Gwen Stefani chose for an outdoor photo op a lacy blue bra barely covered by a loose overall-type garment. And what about all those sports bras worn in public? With bra as the operative word, that makes them an undergarment, not street wear.

Not since Jane Russell's 38 D breasts were seductively displayed in *The Outlaw* has there been so much cleavage in sight. Sadly, much of the *décolletage* is unsightly, over the top if you will, flaunted by wrinkled matrons stuffed like sausages into age-inappropriate tank tops, or by ingénues with grossly enhanced bosoms popping out of dresses a size too small to accommodate the excess *avoirdupois*. The word boobs comes to mind; not in reference to the upper body, but to the young ladies' IQ.

Wearers of a thong panty are easily identified by its elastic peeking above low slung jeans. Gangsta rap hip-hop young males lower their jeans to half mast, revealing designer brand names and the wearers' preferred style of briefs or boxers. Speaking of jeans, let's not forget teenaged starlet Brooke Shields who flirted that nothing came between her and her Calvins. Years later, Britney Spears went Shields one better and allowed paparazzi to prove that nothing came between her and her mini skirt.

I grew up in Iowa, with its bitterly cold winters calling for union suits (long johns) for boys and men, and cotton undershirts for girls, along with full-length brown cotton stockings (white on Sunday). Years later, I insulated my daughter with undershirts, although we lived in warmer Virginia. When she grew up, I forgot about undershirts. I assumed they'd gone the way of corsets and girdles, replaced by training bras for pre-teen girls, an attempt to fast forward them into women before they can spell the word puberty. If there were training bras available in my childhood, I never saw or heard of them. Training pants, yes; those thick pull-ups for toddlers transitioning from diapers to the brave new world.

One winter evening in Virginia, I watched my three young grandkids undress and don pajamas. Is there anything cuter than kids in pajamas? But it was their sleeveless undershirts that caught my eye. My grandson's was blue; the girls' were white with a dainty flower adorning the scoop neckline.

"They're wearing undershirts," I said.

My daughter smiled knowingly, as if this item might not be as popular as it once was, but it was just the ticket for her youngsters.

One day in Target, I stopped in the girls' department to see if they had day-of-the-week underpants for my granddaughters. In my childhood, they came in white or pastel colors with the day of the week embroidered near the leg opening. I found a package, in girly-girl colors and designs, but what grabbed my attention were the tiny bras swinging from hangers. Bras so small they would fit a scrawny six-year-old. The most startling thing was that many of the bras were padded. Perfectly formed teensy cups for those Miley Cyrus wannabes (don't get me started on her). There were also packages of undershirts, now called camisoles or camis, but what little girl is going to choose these when padded bras are available?

Putting bras in their rightful place, on women, Hollywood gossip had it that Howard Hughes created a wired bra for Jane Russell to wear in *The Outlaw*. But she wrote in her autobiography that Hughes's prototype was uncomfortable, so she wore her own bra on the set, with the strap pushed down. You could've fooled me. In photos from that film, there's no evidence of a bra. Russell later appeared in television ads wearing the 18-hour bra "for us full-figured gals." By that time she was not only full on top, but beyond *zaftig* all over. Later, my namesake Madonna introduced the *bustier* to pop music. More recently, Lady Gaga sported an exploding bra at a concert. As humorist Dave Barry says, I'm not making this up.

Frederick Mellinger is credited with designing the first push-up bra, the Rising Star, in 1948. You know him as Mr. Frederick's of Hollywood. He conceived the idea for his lingerie company during World War II. While his buddies decorated their foxholes with pin-up photos of Betty Grable in a one-piece swimsuit, Mellinger had visions of racier sugarplums dancing in his head.

Calvin Klein brought men's undies out in the open with life-sized ads plastered all over Times Square and in magazines. These muscular models are not wearing your grandfather's skivvies. You've ogled them; you know you have.

Speaking of Grandfather, his sleeveless white undershirts were a wardrobe basic in the 20s and 30s. Clark Gable is said to have all but destroyed the production of that item when, in the 1934 movie, *It Happened One Night,* he peeled off his shirt in front of Claudette Colbert and, shockingly, revealed his bare chest. Women swooned and men took their cue from Gable, discarded their undershirts and used them for polishing the car. Today, the classic white undershirt has a negative connotation, wife beater shirt, harkening back to detective magazines and movies when the good guys wore a suit and a hat and the villain wore a white undershirt.

It's difficult to keep up with fashion trends. I'll agree that underwear need not be unmentionable, but by definition shouldn't it be *under?* Maybe leave something to the imagination? After all, in olden days a glimpse of Marilyn Monroe's bare gams under a windblown skirt was all it took to give Tom Ewell *The Seven Year Itch.*

Oh, Auntie Em

Dorothy: Now which way do we go?
Scarecrow: Pardon me, this way is a very nice way.

~ ~ Frank Baum, The Wizard Of Oz

I blame Adam and Eve. If they hadn't eaten the forbidden fruit, God would not have sentenced them and their descendants to a nomadic life. We would all live in Eden, a place so ideal the word travel would never have been coined. But with the couple's eviction, the comings and goings began.

Lot and his family fled Sodom; Noah booked the first cruise; Moses led a tour through the desert and parted the Red Sea so they could keep on trekking. When Naomi decided to leave her village, her daughter-in-law, Ruth, said, "Whither thou goest, I will go," and off they toddled, hand in hand, giddy as teenagers heading for the mall. The Magi saddled their camels and followed a star, and we've been meandering ever since.

We live in America because Columbus (or was it Leif Erickson or Saint Brenden?) discovered a new place for humans to live. Hearing reports of streets paved with gold and a land of milk and honey, folks shouted, "Head 'em up, move 'em out. Go west, young man."

The exodus continued—on foot, by rickshaw, oxcart, ship, boat, ferry, train, horseback, dog sled, prairie schooner, and stagecoach. In time, technology made the automobile the preferred mode of transportation. The fictional Joad family strapped lock, stock and dreams of employment onto their dilapidated vehicle and motored from Oklahoma's dustbowl to California's fertile valleys. A couple decades later, Dinah Shore urged television viewers to *See the U.S.A. in your Chevrolet.* With Dad as pilot, Mom scanned the road map showing the new Interstate highways, read Burma-Shave signs aloud, and periodically answered the kids' question, "When will we get there?"

The James Fitzpatrick Travelogues shown before feature movies in the 1940s sedated me. I came alert only when Fitzpatrick droned, "As the sun sinks slowly into the west, we bid fond adieu to the quaint people of Timbuktu (or wherever his slide show had taken us). His drowsy voice made these sojourns as interminable as the Bataan Death March. Please, bring on the MGM musical.

The family sedan begat the station wagon with luggage racks, which begat tow-behind Silver Stream campers. Today's RVs, so huge they could be recycled into city buses, tow boats, bicycles, motorcycles, and smaller cars for side trips. The vagabond kings and queens of the road who roam in these condos on wheels have their own encampments with catchy names such as Breezy Oaks and Teepee Town. At dusk, the exhilarated travelers gather around an outdoor grill and discuss where they're from, where they've been, and where they're headed.

The world has shrunk to the size of a Swedish meatball. Planes transport us coast to coast in about five hours and to other continents in a few more. But planes have shrunk, too. It's no luxury getting anywhere seated upright in a position that a yoga expert would find uncomfortable. Recline the seat? Right; two inches back makes a huge difference. And convince me that the little belt clipped across my lap will save my life. Flying over water numbs me. I almost drowned as a kid. Floatation device? I don't remember instructions well when I'm in panic mode and the music from *Jaws* is drumming in my ears.

Step into any group of people and you'll hear travel talk: the Alps, the Holy Land, the Amazon, the pyramids. "You'll have to come over," a man says. "I put the photos from our trip around the world into a Power-Point presentation."

He doesn't mention that it runs six hours, thirteen minutes.

Heaven help us if there's an astronaut in the group. How does one top going to the moon?

These magical stories are sprinkled with laments about delayed or missed flights, security snags, lost luggage, jet lag, sea sickness, language misunderstandings, and Montezuma's revenge. Hank had a gall bladder attack and ended up in the hospital. A llama drooled on Ada. Stan left his Kindle on a train in Zurich. Would you believe Max and Irene encountered pirates near their cruise ship? Gee whiz, that was scary. Still, all the trouble is forgotten and plans are underway for the next adventure.

For the record, I appreciate Woody Guthrie's "From California, to the New York Island, From the redwood forest, to the Gulf stream waters ..." I've marveled at spacious skies, amber waves of grain, purple mountains majesty, and fruited plains. I've gotten kicks on Route 66; traveled Blue Highways and new highways, been up North, South of the Border; flown East and West and over the cuckoo's nest. Been around the block and across the pond; been to Europe, the Caribbean, and South Africa—twice. Delved into caves, coves, caverns, canyons, catacombs, and climbed the stairs in the Leaning Tower of Pisa. It's a big, wide, wonderful world, no doubt about it.

But is anyone besides me tired of traipsing all over planet Earth? I understand—it's difficult to admit you enjoy staying home. People think you're missing a cylinder if you don't enjoy traveling. It's chic to travel; it's educational; it's a status symbol; it's … exhausting.

I propose a support group for home-bodies. There would be no meetings to attend. Members would sell their luggage and walking shoes and the polyester wash-and-wear travel clothes. Then relax, read a book, plant a garden, take a nap, watch the grass grow, or put old travel photos in albums and mark them: Been there, done that.

Anything that doesn't require passports, inoculations, or roadmaps would be acceptable activity. Suggested attire is sweat pants and a t-shirt bearing the words: Oh, Auntie Em, there's no place like home.

{ FINALE }

Life Stories

It's wrong to believe that only professional writers can write something of value. I'm trying to convince these groups [family history] that all of the intentions they've had for writing are worthy; and I am here to give them permission to write, as if they need it, though often they do, and to convince them that writing leaves a trace, and there wouldn't be a trace of what they thought or felt or knew about their families, or what they believe about God. There will be no trace of that unless they write it.

~ ~ Charles Baxter

In the end, maybe it is not the absolute truth we seek. Rather, it is the physical proof, a written document, evidence of a life—lively, flawed, joyous.

~ ~ Pamela Gerhardt, *Washington Post* Staff Writer

What we, or at any rate what I, refer to confidently as memory—meaning a moment, a scene, a fact that has been subjected to a fixative and thereby rescued from oblivion—is really a form of storytelling that goes on continually in the mind and often changes with the telling. Too many conflicting emotional interests are involved for life ever to be wholly acceptable, and possibly it is the work of the storyteller to rearrange things so that they conform to this end. In any case, in talking about the past we lie with every breath we take.

~ ~ William Maxwell, *So Long, See You Tomorrow*

Vintage Books, 1980

Have You Read

SWINGING SISTERS

Swinging Sisters is a one-of-a-kind book, because there is no other story like it. Come along for the ride with a Depression era all-girl band as they tour the country in a 1928 Packard hearse. The Texas Rangerettes garner headlines in *Variety* and *Billboard* for several years before taking a fork in the road that subsequently has Paramount Studio cameramen camping on the women's doorstep hoping to film a history-making event featuring four band members.

Based on the true story of my cousins, Mary McLaughlin Jones and her four daughters: Hazel, Gladys, Dorothy, and Evelyn Jones.

Comment on Amazon from Sandra Slate (Middleburg, Florida): I found the book to be delightful, easy reading for when I want to read something light.

MASQUERADE: THE SWINDLER WHO CONNED J. EDGAR HOOVER

The dismal economic times of the 1930s fostered a spree of major and minor crimes, including an army of con men roaming the country. One young Hungarian immigrant's genius for masquerade extended to impersonating noted people in order to prey on industrialists and celebrities. His success prompted J. Edgar Hoover to write in the *American Magazine*, May 1937:

> We sometimes refer to September 28, 1934, as Celebrity Day. That was the date of the great roundup, when we took into custody a German baron, several sons of American ambassadors, a few popular polo players, a member of the Wickersham Committee, a third assistant solicitor general of the United States, an Army colonel, a government undercover man, an around-the-world flier, a motion picture magnate, a number of house guests of industrial giants and multimillionaires, and the manager of the world's biggest doll factory. But this crowd of important men sat in only one chair. They were all represented in the multiple personality of a single individual, George Robert Gabor.

After the imposter's 1936 deportation, Hoover said, "We haven't heard of him again, and we don't want to. But you never can tell." Within months, the Bureau suspected that Gabor had returned, but they failed to find him. In 1942, a clever ruse by the swindler led the FBI to close the case. Hoover never learned that he, too, had been conned.

Comment on Amazon from Chia (Israel): *Masquerade* is very well researched about a man, his time and the ability to pretend and convince others.

DOLLS REMEMBERED

As touchstones to the past, dolls validate childhood, a span of years that often seem like fragmented moments in time. With their life-like faces, blemished complexions, and snarled hair, vintage dolls hold sway with a magical power that rarely wanes, and often grows.

In this collection, 60 contributors reminisce about their childhood dolls. Not all the dolls were pretty; not all were wanted; some were disappointing; not all became favorites, but each doll is memorable.

Comment on Amazon by Ingeborg E. Knight (Florida): The perfect gift from a mother to her daughter and granddaughter. The uniqueness of a doll to a girl is timeless; as being told in this collection of childhood memories.

TOYS REMEMBERED

Although many toys and games are common to a particular era, each boy's experience is unique. The locales in this collection represent a cross-section of America, as well as the Philippines, Canada, England, and Latvia. Some stories are poignant, others are humorous; some are serious, others are tongue-in-cheek; still others slip into fantasy or whimsy, or are creatively dramatized.

The dictionary defines a toy as something a child plays with or uses in play. So, is a stick strummed across a picket fence a toy? When in the hands of children, do maple tree seed pods become toy helicopters? Was the old Underwood typewriter on which Nelle Harper Lee and Truman Persons (later Capote) pecked out stories, a toy? Must a toy be tangible, or might it be as weightless as a whisper secreted in a boy's small fist?

Keep an open mind, for these reminiscences are not only about toys; they are about indoor and outdoor games and the arena in which they were played. In sum, this anthology is about boyhood. One writer called it, "The magic and wonder and marvel of that time of life; the simplicity and innocence of childhood."

Step back and enjoy the magic.

Comment on Amazon by Linus&Bubba Books: Charming, witty, and packed full of nostalgia. A must-read for anyone still in touch with their inner child! Nice quick reads, too.

Meet the Author

Madonna Dries Christensen has won awards and accolades for her writing. Her first published fiction garnered a nomination for the Pushcart Prize. As a novice, she didn't know what that was and had to look it up. Two other nominations followed, one for fiction, one for nonfiction.

Madonna lives beside Worlud Pond in Sarasota, Florida, with her husband, Gary Christensen. She is Editor/Publisher of *Doorways* magazine; a columnist for *Extra Innings*, and Contributing Editor to *Writer's Magazette* and *Yesterday's Magazette*.

Her previous books are: *Swinging Sisters*; *Masquerade: The Swindler Who Conned J. Edgar Hoover; The Quiet Warrior*; *Dolls Remembered*, and *Toys Remembered*. All books are available through Amazon and other major bookstores. Royalties go to chosen organizations.

Web site: www.madonnadrieschristensen.com.

Piece by piece: The image on the jigsaw puzzle mentioned earlier was a male lion sprawled on a rocky ledge. The lion and the ledge were the same tawny color, making the puzzle difficult to complete. MDC

Sibley, Iowa, circa 1947: The author and her mother